TODAY'S LONDON OVERGROUND
A PICTORIAL OVERVIEW

For Vicky
An incredibly patient wife!

TODAY'S LONDON OVERGROUND
A PICTORIAL OVERVIEW

JUSTIN BAILEY

PEN & SWORD TRANSPORT

AN IMPRINT OF PEN & SWORD BOOKS LTD.
YORKSHIRE – PHILADELPHIA

First published in Great Britain in 2021 by
Pen and Sword Transport
An imprint of
Pen & Sword Books Ltd.
Yorkshire - Philadelphia

Copyright © Justin Bailey, 2021

ISBN 978 1 52677 262 6

The right of Justin Bailey to be identified as author of this work has been
asserted by him in accordance with the Copyright, Designs and Patents Act 1988.

A CIP catalogue record for this book is available from the British Library.

All rights reserved. No part of this book may be reproduced or transmitted in any form or
by any means, electronic or mechanical including photocopying, recording or by any
information storage and retrieval system, without permission from the Publisher in writing.

Typeset in Minion Pro by SJmagic DESIGN SERVICES, India

Printed and bound in India by Replika Press Pvt. Ltd.

Pen & Sword Books Ltd incorporates the Imprints of Pen & Sword Books Archaeology, Atlas, Aviation, Battleground, Discovery, Family History, History, Maritime, Military, Naval, Politics, Railways, Select, Transport, True Crime, Fiction, Frontline Books, Leo Cooper, Praetorian Press, Seaforth Publishing, Wharncliffe and White Owl.

For a complete list of Pen & Sword titles please contact

PEN & SWORD BOOKS LIMITED
47 Church Street, Barnsley, South Yorkshire, S70 2AS, England
E-mail: enquiries@pen-and-sword.co.uk
Website: www.pen-and-sword.co.uk

or

PEN AND SWORD BOOKS
1950 Lawrence Rd, Havertown, PA 19083, USA
E-mail: Uspen-and-sword@casematepublishers.com
Website: www.penandswordbooks.com

Contents

Chapter 1	The London Overground: A Short History	7
Chapter 2	Clapham Junction	12
Chapter 3	East London Line: Highbury and Islington to New Cross/New Cross Gate	16
	East London Line Extension, New Cross Gate to West Croydon and Crystal Palace	36
Chapter 4	Gospel Oak to Barking Line	45
Chapter 5	Lea Valley Lines: London Liverpool Street to Enfield Town and Cheshunt	64
Chapter 6	Lea Valley Lines: Liverpool Street to Chingford	85
Chapter 7	North London Line	96
Chapter 8	Romford to Upminster	119
Chapter 9	South London Line	123
Chapter 10	Watford DC Lines	131
Chapter 11	West London Line	152
Chapter 12	Willesden Junction	159
Chapter 13	London Overground Signage	165
Chapter 14	Overground Named Trains	172
Bibliography		176

Chapter One

The London Overground: A Short History

The Orange Line, the Ginger Line, the London orbital railway, the M25 railway, call it what you will. The London Overground has grown from an amalgamation of lines (including a former London Underground one) and railway companies to become a railway company with an identity in its own right. And with a few hiccups (some larger than others in the case of the Gospel Oak route), it has gone on to become something of a transport success story, serving London and its outlying areas since 2007. An orbital railway around London is not a new idea, however. Both the London North Western and London Midland Railways had outer circle routes around London as far back as the late 1800s. Both of them were short-lived. But it could be argued that the genesis of today's modern London Overground goes back to 1974 with the advent of the *Barren Report*. This suggested some kind of joined-up rail network, using lines situated, in most part, north of the River Thames But improvements were few and far between, with projects carried out in the late 1970s and mid '80s by the Greater London Council (GLC) to improve services on the North London Line. When British Rail's London and Southeastern arm, Network SouthEast (NSE), was set up in 1982, improvements continued still further. Also, 'passenger power' of volunteer interest groups and political advocacy groups began to put forward ideas of their own. With the help of the newly formed Greater London Authority (GLA), the successor to the GLC in 2000, one of these ideas concentrated on better links in South London, traditionally poorly served by London Underground. Using the North Kent Lines and routes in the south west of the capital, this bore fruit in the shape of the 'ON-overground network' initiative in 2003. While mainly a branding exercise between the Strategic Rail Authority, (SRA) Transport for London (TfL) and Southern/South Western train operating companies, it helped influence better services in the south of the capital until its demise in 2006, a year before 'London Overground' was launched. Similarities may be noted between the name of the two and the orange colour used by both in their visual branding.

Interestingly, the idea of bringing the south London railway routes used in the 'overground network' exercise under TfL/London Overground control, and out of the hands of their constituent franchises, is still being argued for to this day. When Britain's railway network was privatised in 1996, many of the rail routes around London were taken over by Silverlink Metro, owned by National Express. This again saw limited improvement, though many would say only superficial improvement at that. But the concept of an orbital railway around the capital was still promoted officially from 2001 and was something that the GLA was keen to get started on. By 2004, TfL had been granted powers over some rail services in and around London and they would begin with the Silverlink Metro services in 2007.

For it was in 2007 that Silverlink Trains, an operator of mainly North London rail lines, passed into history in yet another shakeup of the railway franchise map. Its London Metro routes were passed onto a new company that would come under the umbrella of TfL, and 'London Overground' was born. These original routes were the North London Line, the West London Line, the Watford DC Line and the Gospel Oak to Barking Line (otherwise known as the 'GOBLIN'). Looking at these on a map, you would see that this pretty much covered the top half of the capital, with two forays across the Thames at Richmond and Clapham Junction in the south. Stations on these routes were refurbished and new trains were rolled out, replacing ageing units. In keeping with the rest of TfL's varying methods of transport, the branding was uniform in its appearance alongside that of the Tube and Bus network, although the identifying colour, inherited from the East London Line, was orange. The next evolution of the Overground story comes with the passing into history of one of London Underground's most famous routes, the East London Line, which closed at the end of 2007. It reopened in 2010 after refurbishment and rebuilding as part of the London Overground. By now, the line had been extended as far as Dalston Junction in the north and then further still to Highbury and Islington, linking it to the North London Line by 2011. In the south, it was extended beyond the line's original terminus at New Cross Gate as far as Norwood Junction, West Croydon and Crystal Palace, with the short branch to New Cross still remaining. Next came the extension over large parts of the South London Line, which was known as Phase 2 of the East London Line extension to Clapham Junction, where it met the Overground section of the West London Line. All of this was done using a mix of old and new infrastructure, so the London Overground wasn't just absorbing current lines, but also now building new and reusing disused ones. By now, the London Overground had truly become an orbital London railway, taking in points north, east, south and west. But the story doesn't end there, for in mid-2015, former Greater Anglia routes out of London Liverpool Street to Enfield Town, Cheshunt and Chingford were taken over as well. For the train enthusiast, these routes could be viewed as being of more interest, as at the time of writing, ageing Electric Multiple Units inherited from the previous franchise were still running on these lines in London Overground colours. And lastly, something of a curio on the London Overground map is the short three-station line between Romford and Upminster, isolated and all on its own.

So what of the future? The short extension from Barking to Barking Riverside is underway with a hoped for opening date of 2021/22. After that, another popular idea is the WLO (West London Orbital) from Hounslow to Hampstead Heath over some of the little-used freight-only Dudding Hill Line in West London, via Old Oak Common. There has also been recent talk of taking the Greenford Shuttle from Greenford to West Ealing under TfL/Overground control. This might happen in 2021 when the Great Western franchise is reviewed, as it is one of their (lesser known) routes. It used to run all the way to Paddington before Crossrail absorbed this stretch. Of course, this is all far off in the future and things can change rapidly.

This book comes at a time of another round of great change in the short history of the London Overground. As old rolling stock has been phased out, new rolling stock has been phased in. This, and the long campaign of electrifying the Gospel Oak to Barking Line, has tested the Overground network in recent years. But we now have a comprehensive London orbital rail network with a service pattern of every 15 mins on most of its routes, covering more than a hundred miles and over a hundred stations. It has grown to be more than just complementary to London Underground in what has been quite a short space of time.

This book is primarily a photographic record of the London Overground over these past few years, with some photos going back to its introduction and early days. As a point of note, whenever the word 'Overground' is mentioned in this work, it pertains to the London Overground, not any other railway franchised company that runs *overground*. (!) Chapters can be found on each of the routes, including the rolling stock and the stations, with a brief history of each line. The photos for this book were taken mostly in daylight, with some at night, and in all weathers! The majority of pictures were taken before the coronavirus pandemic in 2020. Pictures taken after this to complete this work were taken when the lockdown was being relaxed and I followed strict guidelines by wearing a face mask and using ample amounts of sanitiser at all times! While not every station might be covered, I visited all 112 of them, (including Battersea Park!), sometimes two or even three times. I have tried to work on this book from the perspective of the railway enthusiast, as being one myself I wanted to show what an enthusiast can see and photograph (with a couple of exceptions). I have used a variety of digital cameras over the years, including two Fuji 'Bridge' cameras and two SLRs, one Sony and a Canon. As so much of the London Overground network is shared by freight trains, some shots of these have also been included. All of the sources and reference works I used for research can be found in the bibliography at the end of the book. And though I have to admit that I used Wikipedia on occasion, and Google Maps was very, very helpful, the London & South East Rail Services map was always by my side.

I hope you enjoy the book!

Justin Bailey,
Middlesex, 2021

Full credit for this amazing London Overground Map with amendments for possible copyright reasons goes to 'sameboat' from wikimedia commons

Chapter Two

Clapham Junction

Clapham Junction, one of the busiest stations in Europe, is the interchange point on the London Overground between the South/East London Line and the West London Line. It also serves South West Railways trains out of London Waterloo and Southern Rail services out of Victoria, seeing in excess of 120 trains an hour. Interestingly, it's named not after one particular junction but because it's the junction of a whole number of junctions. The station itself is numbered from Platforms 1 to 17. West London Line services, the precursor to half of the Overground services at Clapham Junction, used Platforms 1 & 2 and 16 & 17 until 1965. When, after this, Clapham Junction 'A' Box suffered a structural failure, they could only use 16 & 17. Years later they returned to Platform 2 only, as in 1980, Platform 1 had been taken out of service. When the London Overground South/East London Line was extended to Clapham Junction in 2012, Platform 2 was rebuilt to have a new bay platform 'knocked into it'. This became the new Platform 1. The old Platform 1 alongside is still trackless but may well see service in the future as Platform 0! West London Line Overground services now use the new Platform 1, and South/East London line services use Platform 2 further up. Passengers in a hurry need to check upon reaching the bottom of the staircase from the footbridge or up from the subway that they alight onto the correct train. The one on the left goes west, the one on the right goes south! Though as the author has found out himself, in times of engineering work or trouble at Clapham Junction, Platform 17 is still used for Overground Services. This can result in a mad headlong dash by hundreds of waiting passengers from one side of the station to the other, either by the subway or the bridge!

9 January 2010 and the London Overground is three years old as 378 015 in the original 3-car formation pulls into a snow-covered Clapham Junction, having arrived from the West London Line. It's arriving at the old Platform 2 before the South/East London Line extension forced a change to the numbering here. (*Sony A100*)

17 January 2010 and the winter sun is reflected off the front of 378 011 as it climbs up the approach into Platform 17 on the far side of Clapham Junction. Clapham Junction 'B' Signal Box is to the left, having been decommissioned in 1985. To the right of it can also be seen Battersea's blue MAN gasholder, demolished in 2017. (*Sony A100*)

2 July 2019 and 378 139 leaves the 'new' Platform 2 in the distance under the footbridge bound for the South/East London Line. It's passing 378 220, which is sitting at the 'new' Platform 1 to and from the West London Line, that's been cut into the old Platform 2. (*Fuji X-S1*)

2 July 2019. No.378 150 approaches Platform 2 at Clapham Junction having come from the South/East London Line. It's wearing the revised London Overground livery that was being introduced in late 2018. This new livery was slow to be rolled out, such was the need to keep as much of the 378 fleet in service at any one time, especially with the shortage of rolling stock on the Gospel Oak to Barking Line. (*Fuji X-S1*)

19 November 2019, the re-liveried 378 150 again at the 'new' Platform 2, Clapham Junction, this time in the evening rush hour. The head height platform fencing in front of the cab ostensibly separates Platform 2 from the 'new' Platform 1 to the right, out of shot. On its platform side signs indicate which train is for the West London Line and which train is for the South/East London line, as both are parked almost in front of each other. (*Fuji X-S1*)

4 February 2017 and an unidentified London Overground class 378 sits at the 'new' Platform 2, Clapham Junction. The sign on Platforms 5 & 6 claims that Clapham Junction is Britain's busiest railway station. As a lad growing up, the author was always informed by his father that it was one of the busiest in the world! I'm not sure how true that was then, but it now sees more than 120 trains an hour from South Western Railways, Southern and London Overground, with the Gatwick Express and freight passing through. (*Fuji X-S1*)

29 January 2020, and 378 225 sits at Platform 17, having been diverted from its normal terminating point on Platform 1, because of points trouble in the evening rush hour. The passengers packing the platform have just rushed all the way over from Platform 1 by subway and footbridge. They wait to board with many more behind them while other passengers struggle to get off. When the author finally managed to get on board he found the front three coaches packed to the doors, but the last two all but empty, as passengers had refused to move down in a walk-through train! (*Canon 750d*)

Chapter Three

East London Line

Highbury and Islington to New Cross/New Cross Gate

The East London Line (ELL) has a few distinctions on the London Overground network. Firstly, it was the only line taken over by the Overground that was formerly a London Underground route. Secondly, aside from the electrification of the GOBLIN, it's seen more investment and rebuilding than any of the other routes. And thirdly, through its extensions and rebuilding, it is the only Overground route that has properly reached south of the river (so far!) In its earliest form under the East London Railway consortium, it ran from New Cross and New Cross Gate in the south, through East London and under the Thames via I. K. Brunel's historic Thames Tunnel. Continuing on via Whitechapel and Shoreditch, it terminated at Liverpool Street. This provided a cross-London link for various Southern Railway companies and freight to the Great Eastern. The Underground got involved when the line was linked to the fledging underground network via a subterranean connection west of Whitechapel at St Marys for Metropolitan and District line services in 1884. Electrification using the four rail system followed in 1913. After 1933, passenger services were solely run by the Underground, except for specials and excursion traffic. Run as the East London branch of the Metropolitan Line, underground services to Hammersmith were withdrawn by 1941, though the line was still connected to the Underground network for empty stock movements. On the map the route then took on the appearance of a short, isolated branch of the Underground. The stretch between Shoreditch and Liverpool Street then ceased in 1966 when freight services over it were discontinued and track was taken up. In the 1980s, it gained its own identity as the East London Line. It then got its own orange colour on the map in the 1990s, the route using Metropolitan line tube stock. This is the colour that would define the Overground network in its future. In 1995, the entire line closed completely for major upgrade work, with a new station at Canada Water and a Jubilee Line interchange being started. While the line was shut, major refurbishment work could also be done on its historic Thames Tunnel, opened in 1843, which was seeing rather more water ingress than was liked.

It was then, however, that the East London Line faced perhaps its greatest challenge yet. With hours to go before the line was due to be closed, English Heritage, in an amazing piece of timing, got the Thames Tunnel Grade II listed. You might well ask why it took them so long, and why only Grade II, considering its importance to the engineering world. But anyone with a little knowledge of the 'listing' process of buildings will appreciate the ramifications this would go on to have. The original plans for the refurbishment of the tunnel, including 'shotcreting' its walls and ceiling, became redundant overnight. Options were then floated around as to what to do about this dilemma. Building a new tunnel or complete closure of the line were mooted, the former being more fantastical (and unlikely) than the latter, considering the cost. Eventually, English Heritage came to a compromise with London Underground and work was started. In the end the length of closure for the line planned at seven months ended up taking until 1998. The Thames Tunnel was refurbished to a more 'sympathetic' design with some of the original architecture untouched. Needless to say, this did not do the budget, or the patience of its passengers (using rail replacement buses for three years), any good whatsoever. But it was also during this refurbishment that the public was granted rare access over the course of some weekends to walk the tunnel on ticketed guided tours. The author was offered a spare ticket by a friend and took many pictures, some of which are included in this book. The new station at Canada Water, with its Jubilee Line connection below, was then opened in 1999. Then in 2006 the line contracted again with the closure of Shoreditch station at the eastern end of the line, one of the least used on the network. This was in preparation for the Overground takeover. This briefly made Whitechapel the new terminus. So, at 4.5 miles long, this was the East London line until 2007 when it passed into history and closed for good, passing over to London Overground for major rebuilding.

And contrary to its contraction in past years, the New East London Line has seen massive expansion, known as the ELLX (East London Line Extension). The first phase, Phase 1, was to link it up to the North London Line in the north and to West Croydon and Crystal Palace in the south. The Northern extension was done by extending the route over most of the 2.5 mile long Kingsland viaduct that once carried the North London line into the old Broadstreet station that was not far away. A new elevated station called Shoreditch High Street was built on the site of the old Bishopsgate Goods complex, as the old Shoreditch station was at a different level where alignment was unsuitable. Further new stations were built at Hoxton, Haggerston and Dalston Junction along the viaduct. The latter two replaced previous stations closed when the line to Broadstreet Station closed in 1986. The new station at Dalston Junction was a big undertaking as most of it is underground and it has two terminating and two through lines. Extending further north, the line then links up to the North London Line at Canonbury before terminating at Highbury and Islington, where the DC third rail ends.

In the south, the short branch to New Cross was kept and the line was extended beyond its terminus at New Cross Gate to Norwood Junction, West Croydon and Crystal Palace. A new bridge was built at New Cross Gate to take London bound services over the Brighton Mainline and new track laid through the station beyond the previous stops. A major Overground Traction Maintenance Depot serving the South and East London Overground Lines was built here as well. The rest of the route south used existing lines running parallel with the above mentioned Southern-operated mainline. Phase 1 was completed in 2010 after which the East London Line formally became part of the London Overground.

Phase 2 of the ELLX saw the line connect to the South London Line to Clapham Junction, via a disused East London Railway trackbed. Major infrastructure had to be built here at Silwood Junction outside Surrey Quays so that northbound services from New Cross and the south could cross over the top of Clapham-bound South London Line services, negating the use of a flat junction. This last phase was completed by the end of 2012 which meant that the final gap in the Overground's route around London had been closed and the orbit now completed. By changing trains at Clapham Junction and Highbury and Islington, passengers could now circumnavigate the capital entirely on London Overground!

11 July 2019. We start our journey down the East London Line (ELL) at the end of the line here at Highbury and Islington. A class 378 leaves the station on the North London Line side, heading west past the point where the tracks of the East London Line come to an end. Curiously, the line on Platform 1 of the ELL has retained its DC third rail all the way to the buffer stops (though not used for a long time by the looks of it), while the line on Platform 2, despite losing its third rail back in the platform behind the photographer, continues on beyond the bridge in the distance. (*Fuji X-S1*)

Passengers rush down the stairs of the footbridge to board 378 153 before it leaves for its journey down the East London Line, while another 378 has arrived at Platform 8 on the North London Line side. The headlights of another 378 can be seen arriving under the main station building at the top of the picture. Platforms 1 & 2 were, for some years, the original North London Line platforms before the East London Line was extended here, taking them over instead. Confusing the issue is that the current North London Lines are often referred to as the 'No.1 Lines'! Platforms 3, 4, 5 & 6 are below ground on the Great Northern and London Underground Victoria Lines. (*Fuji X-S1*)

6 July 2019. Canonbury Station marks the first true interchange with the North London Line travelling west. During an overcast summer's day, a 378 in the new London Overground livery arrives at Platform 2. Unit numbers were progressively moved from the cab front to below the cab door on the side as the new livery was rolled out on these units making identification difficult in pictures such as this. Note also the raised part of the platforms to bring them level with the floor height of the train, about to be taken advantage of by the gentleman pushing the buggy. Another effort to make the London Overground as accessible as possible. (*Fuji X-S1*)

11 July 2019. Deep under Dalston is the new Dalston Junction Station, opened in 2010. Though built on the site of the former above-ground North London Line station that closed on the route to Broad Street in 1986, it's been enclosed in a 'subterranean' type box. This was done so a major housing development could be built above it, maximising land value. A double-track central bay terminating platform, occupied by 378 148 and 378 233 (just arrived), is flanked by two through-running lines on either side. (*Fuji X-S1*)

11 July 2019. No. 378 224 approaches Dalston Junction down the impressive incline from Haggerston Station in the distance. This stretch and its approaches to Dalston Junction make heavy use of slab track as seen in the picture. This type of permanent way is often used to reduce maintenance, be more load-bearing and to ensure as little movement as possible of the track formation over time. It also has noise deadening properties as well. All important things to consider in the confines of such a route as this, especially with so much housing above. (*Fuji X-S1*)

13 June 2020. Compare this image to a view of what Dalston Junction Station would have looked like back in the 1960s, or even in the early 1980s, just before closure, and it would be unrecognisable now. Taken from the Richmond Road Bridge a class 378 leaves from the station heading to one of four destinations: New Cross, Crystal Palace, West Croydon or Clapham Junction. Because of this, there is on average a train passing through or leaving every 5–10 minutes. (*Canon 750d*)

11 July 2019. No. 378 215 crests the rise into Haggerston Station in a shot that gives a good indication of the climb out of Dalston Junction. The white and brown buildings seen behind the colour light signal is the housing development that was built on top of the new Dalston Junction Station, including Sledge Tower being the tallest amongst them. (*Fuji X-T1*)

13 June 2020. The new Haggerston Station must stand out on the East London Line as one of the most architecturally pleasing. Designed by railway infrastructure architects Acanthus Architects LW, it was meant to echo the style of Charles Holden who designed so many of the London Underground's famous stations. The old station was situated further south, but closed in 1940, prior to being heavily damaged by bombing in the Second World War rather than as a result of it! (*Canon 750d*)

11 July 2019. Newly liveried 378 135 runs into Hoxton Station along the Kingsland Viaduct. This viaduct is approximately two miles in length and spans East London from the City of London to Dalston. It was the major piece of infrastructure that carried the original North London Line from Broad Street Station to Dalston Junction until the line was closed in 1986. (*Fuji X-S1*)

11 July 2019. Hoxton Station seen from up above at Platform level. This was the only entirely new station to be built on this stretch, as it never existed before on this original stretch of the North London Line. The high screens on the sides of both platforms help mitigate passengers being blown about too much on this elevated station. (*Fuji X-S1*)

13 June 2020. Hoxton Station as seen from ground level, set in the arches of the Kingsland Viaduct. Also located here, just behind the lift staircase tower in the background, is the North London Railway war memorial. First situated on the concourse of Broad Street Station, it was saved when that station was demolished. It then found a home at Richmond Station at the end of the North London Line, before being relocated here in 2010 and rededicated in 2011. Despite this now being an East London Line station, it was formally on North London Line territory, so having the memorial here so close to its original home makes sense. (*Canon 750d*)

18 September 2010. The early morning light catches the city of London as 378 150 approaches Haggerston. This was the view that you used to be able to get from the end of Platform 2. But such has been the pace of change in the city over recent years that when the author returned almost 10 years later, he found that this scene had been altered somewhat for the worse. More developments of apartments and flats having been built behind the viaduct have obscured everything up to the top of the church spire. (Sony A100)

18 September 2010. During the popular annual London 'Open House' event in 2010, the owners of the Bishopsgate Complex opened one of the upper floors of the Broadgate Tower to the public. Such were the views that the author queued up twice to go up, as time at the top was limited to 10 minutes per group! This picture, taken then, gives a wonderful view of the ELL Extension, complete with a 4-car 378. The new viaduct curving in from Shoreditch on the right meets the old Kingsland Viaduct on its way north. Another part of the old viaduct can be seen in the foreground, complete with 1983 Jubilee Line tube stock hoisted onto it, now used as offices! The author is literally standing on the site of the old Broad Street Station, but much higher up! (Sony A100)

13 June 2020. Two class 378s cross on the bowstring bridge that crosses Shoreditch High Street outside the station of the same name. This is one of two similar bridges built on the ELL northern extension, the second being across the Regents Canal between Hoxton and Haggerston. The preponderance of street art in the area can be seen, similar to Hackney Wick. (*Canon 750d*)

18 September 2010. This view taken from Braithwaite Street in 2010 shows the new Shoreditch Station on the right, built in a long elevated box that looks, from some angles, like a huge alligator sitting in Shoreditch. It was built on the remains of what was previously the old Bishopsgate Goods Yard that closed after a fire in 1964, the retaining walls of which can be seen on the left. Some of the remains of the old goods yard, the Braithwaite Arches, were listed as being some of the oldest railway infrastructure in the world. However, a lot of what used to be here in the picture was sadly demolished to make way for this new station after a bitter legal battle in 2003. (*Sony A100*)

11 July 2019. Inside the long 'box on legs' of the new Shoreditch High Street London Overground Station. The old Shoreditch station on the London Underground East London Line isn't far away. But being little used in its later years, it closed for good in 2006, two years before the East London Underground line closed and passed over to London Overground. It would also have been in the wrong place and too small for the ELL Extension in any case. Being built enclosed like this means that any future development around the station will have minimal impact on its day to day operation. (*Fuji X-S1*)

18 September 2010. No. 378 141 has just crossed the new bridge built over Shoreditch High Street and is about to enter Shoreditch High Street Station. The sharp curve out of the station here, across the new bridge, was necessary so the new alignment on a new viaduct could meet the remains of the Kingsland Viaduct. This new viaduct, seen in the previous aerial view, and this new station, were some of the largest pieces of infrastructure and investment made on the whole of the East London Line Northern Extension. (*Sony A100*)

13 June 2020. A shot taken from behind the end of the original Shoreditch London Underground station building that closed for good in 2006. No. 378 142 climbs the new alignment and is about to cross the bridge that takes the ELL Northern Extension over the Great Eastern Mainline out of Liverpool Street. This new incline was one of the most substantial pieces of infrastructure on the new East London Line, being built on top of the filled-in cutting that used to take the ELL, under its previous London Underground incarnation, to its terminus just a feet away from this spot. (*Canon 750d*)

19 June 2020. Whitechapel station is one of only two places on the Overground network where the Underground crosses over it (on the District and Hammersmith Circle Lines). However, since work commenced to build a new station interchange above the rebuilt Underground station, for the new Crossrail station below the Overground station, Whitechapel Station has been one big building site for a few years! Effectively, it will be three stations above each other with a new concourse on top. Challenging, to say the least. On the northbound platform a passenger reads a poster depicting what the new station will look like. Quite something if pictures are anything to go by. (*Canon 750d*)

13 June 2020. Re-liveried 378 206 comes to a stand in Shadwell Station beneath the extra bracing and supports on the retaining walls that help keep the station as rigid as possible. This is a feature among the stations on this stretch of the route that was built using the 'cut and cover' method of construction. Open sections can still be found at street level before passing into tunnel again. Building this particular station over a natural spring complicated matters still further. (*Canon 750d*)

13 June 2020. Wapping Station, looking back in the direction of Shadwell with the entrances to Brunel's Thames Tunnel heading south behind the author. This is one of the most cramped stations on the route. The narrow platforms are limited to four coach lengths, so when the class 378 stock arrives, the doors on the rear carriage, still in the tunnel, are locked out of use. With the walk-through nature of these trains, this is of little impediment to the passenger. The station was refurbished during the London Overground take-over, but the pictures on the walls depicting the local area and the line in days of steam, date from the London Underground refurbishment in the 1990s, and have been kept. (*Canon 750d*)

13 June 2020. Wapping station seen from street level. The original station was badly damaged in the war and passengers had to make do with a wooden hut for 20 years until a more substantial structure was built. The rotunda caps the original shaft to the tunnels below, while the current station building around it dates from 1982. Under London Overground the entrance was moved from the corner to the front. Note how the new development looming over the station had to be built around it, the shaft being immovable! Going by the flower boxes and hanging baskets, the station is obviously well looked after. (*Canon 750d*)

13 March 2010. With a month to go before the East London Line reopened under London Overground ownership, the public had a very rare opportunity to walk Brunel's world famous Thames Tunnel on some guided tours. The author was kindly given a ticket for one of these tours from a photography friend and took many photos of varying quality in the very dark conditions. This was one of the best, in the right-hand bore looking north towards Wapping. Fortunately, most of the character of the tunnel was kept during its mid-1990s protracted refurbishment. It was the world's first tunnel under a navigable river and was begun by Marc Isambard Brunel in 1825 before being completed by his son Isambard Kingdom Brunel in 1843. It sits 75 feet under the River Thames at its deepest point and is 1,300 feet long. (*Sony A100*)

13 March 2010. Another shot taken on the same special tour, but looking back towards Rotherhithe Station in the more conventional stretch of tunnel, before the more iconic twin bores are reached. Rotherhithe Station is still being fitted out in London Overground style for its reopening in about a month from when this shot was taken. Needless to say, the tours sold out very quickly, taking place over a couple of weekends. Guided and escorted from Rotherhithe Station, groups were taken down one bore to Wapping Station before coming back in the adjacent bore. Unbeknownst to the author at the time was that his future wife was one of the guides taking people through the tunnels! (*Sony A100*)

18 July 2019. Rotherhithe Station building at street level. The original station building had an extension built on the front of it in 1905 to bring it into uniformity with surrounding buildings. Under London Overground ownership, the entrance was also widened by turning the windows either side of the doorway into part of the main entrance itself. The Brunel Museum, showing the history of the tunnel and how it was built, is located up Railway Avenue on the right, in the Brunel Engine House next to the original access shaft. It's well worth a visit. (*Fuji X-S1*)

14 July 2019. Canada Water was an entirely new station built on the London Underground Jubilee Line extension between 1995 and 1999. As the East London Line had an interchange here, it too had to be rebuilt and incorporated into the new station. The original brick tunnel of the ELL was dismantled and the line was laid into a new concrete box with a new station and platforms built around it. Interestingly, the sign for the Jubilee Line platforms indicates for passengers to go up and yet they are situated beneath the East London Line! (*Fuji X-S1*)

18 July 2019. No. 378 137 comes out of the tunnel mouth at Surrey Quays station. As with many tunnels on the route, slab track is used as the norm to damp down noise, maintenance needs and any movement. On the vacant land to the left sat a siding that, in the 1920s, was home to an ice and snow clearing train that cleaned the conductor rails. (*Fuji X-S1*)

18 July 2019. A view of Surrey Quays station shot from Cope Street road bridge as two class 378s pass each other. The station originally opened in 1869 as Deptford Road, but later had its name changed to Surrey Docks to better reflect the area in which it's located. It was renamed Surrey Quays in 1989 when the docks fell into decline. It's an interesting station as it's beneath a skew bridge that carries the Lower Road/A200 across it, the street level buildings being supported on iron columns. (*Fuji X-S1*)

5 September 2010. One of the earliest photos the author took of the Overground is this shot of 378 147 at the stops at New Cross station, five months after London Overground took over this stretch of the East London Line. This platform would have seen many types of London Underground stock in its days as a London Underground destination. The train is a 3-car, but as train lengths have increased on the Overground network, the platform has been altered at the far end. (*Sony A100*)

18 July 2019. No. 378 15? crosses over the new flyover that was built to carry the northbound East London Line from New Cross and New Cross Gate over the southbound ELL extension to the South London Line and Clapham Junction. In the background, another 378 can be seen heading towards New Cross or New Cross Gate. The line on the right is the line from Clapham Junction via the old South London Line. This junction, now called Silwood Junction, was formally known as Deptford Road Junction and was rebuilt after last seeing passenger use in 1913. (*Fuji X-S1*)

17 August 2019. Re-liveried 378 136 arrives at New Cross Gate, about to enter Platform 1. The line on the left is a shunting and stabling turnback that leads back into the London Overground depot at New Cross, which can just be seen in the background. Beyond that can be seen the chimney and the main building for the South East London Combined Heat and Power Plant. (*Canon 750d*)

20 June 2020. While extending the Overground further south from New Cross Gate, it was relatively straightforward by restabilising the connection from Platform 1 beyond the station onto the down slow lines. But going north was a completely different matter. A new bridge and its approach ramp over the Brighton mainline had to be built to take the Overground east, to link it up with its southbound line. Here, 378 143 crosses the bridge with the Overground depot at New Cross on the far right. (*Canon 750d*)

7 February 2020. New Cross Gate station underwent a lot of rebuilding for the coming of the London Overground in 2010. It was modernised with a new cross platform interchange, staircases and lifts. Platform 1, used for Overground services heading south, was refurbished and extended beyond the station to link up with the Southern slow lines to Norwood Junction and Crystal Palace. This was re-establishing a link here that was severed in 1972. Platform 2 is used for southbound Southern services and the island Platforms 3 & 4 are rarely used. Platform 5 is used for northbound Southern and Overground services. (*Canon 750d*)

19 June 2020. New Cross Gate station at street level, similar in appearance to its neighbour, New Cross, before its station buildings were demolished and replaced with a new building in 1975. This station, however, has largely stood the test of time, is a little shorter, and with new entrances at the far end. The current building dates from the mid-1800s, after which it was enlarged and altered twice. (*Canon 750d*)

East London Line Extension, New Cross Gate to West Croydon and Crystal Palace

17 August 2019. No. 378 150, one of the first 378s to gain the new livery, is about to come to a stop at Brockley Station, the first station on the East London Line Southern Extension using the Southern slow lines. The two middle lines are the up and down Brighton fast lines and the line on the far left is the up slow line. The black bridge at the top of the picture is for the Southeastern line from Lewisham to London Victoria via Denmark Hill. (*Canon 750d*)

17 August 2019. Southern EMU 377 604 powers past 378 215 at Honor Oak Park. The station opened in 1886 and was in part funded by local developers who, no doubt, sought a return on their investment in the passengers that the new station would bring into the area. The station hasn't changed much except for the addition of lifts down to platform level. Half hourly Southern services also stop at this Overground station to and from London Bridge, continuing as far as Coulsdon Town. (*Canon 750d*)

17 August 2019. No. 378 146 enters Forest Hill Station while a Southern class 455 has just left, bound for London Victoria or London Bridge on its half hourly stopping service. Forest Hill received severe damage during an air raid in 1944 that destroyed the main station and surrounding buildings. Economies since then have left it with a much smaller, almost prefabricated style building, on the up platform. Note the classic Southern Region concrete signal gantry. (*Canon 750d*)

17 August 2019. Overground 378 142 sits at Sydenham Station on the down platform while Southern 455 807 sits at the up platform. With approximately 27 years difference between them in age, the styles are noticeable. The 378s were purpose built for the Overground network while the 455s were a BR Design built to work on the Southern Region. Now used by South West Railways and Southern, the Southern variants have had the cab gangways plated over to aid air conditioning in the cab. (*Canon 750d*)

17 August 2019. The first of two termini on the ELL Southern Extension can be found here at Crystal Palace having branched off the route to Norwood Junction and West Croydon after Sydenham Station. Overground services here terminate in the formerly disused bay Platform 3 on the left (through Platforms 1 & 2 are behind the wall on the left), or in a newly built bay Platform 5. The new central platform here was built on some disused sidings. The rather short overall roof, while no doubt of some benefit to passengers, is not entirely in keeping with the rest of the station and was added in 2015. No. 378 223 sits between two Southern class 455s waiting to leave. (*Canon 750d*)

17 August 2019. Crystal Palace Station seen from street level. Crystal Palace had two major stations built for the Crystal Palace exhibition after it was moved from Hyde Park. The one pictured was known as Crystal Palace Low Level while another station, built a little closer to Crystal Palace, was called Crystal Palace High Level. This was a grand six-platform station in a huge train shed that closed in 1954, after a decline in passengers that began when the Palace famously burnt down in 1936. The current station, now without its 'High Level' suffix, has been progressively restored since 2002. A 1980s glass booking hall on the side, echoing the design of the Palace, was demolished when the main station building reopened as such in 2012. (*Canon 750d*)

17 August 2019. Crystal Palace Station as seen looking out from the walkway above the platforms. A lot of improvements that were instigated in 2012 saw lift access to all platforms (one can be seen on the far left) and other remedial work undertaken around the station. As some platforms were brought back into use and others rebuilt, they had to be renumbered from 3 onwards. No. 378 223 sits in the new bay Platform 5 waiting to leave for its journey back into East London. (*Canon 750d*)

1 February 2020. Looking northwards towards London, 378 230 has just left Penge West on the up slow line while Southern EMU 377 606 heads south towards West Croydon on the down fast line. The bridge at the top of the picture carries the Overground line to Crystal Palace over these lines. As mentioned in an earlier photo, the Southern Region concrete colour light signal gantry is very prominent in the picture. (*Canon 750d*)

7 February 2020. An Overground 378 passes behind Penge West station high up the line to Crystal Palace. Opened as just Penge in 1839, it closed in 1841 before reopening as Penge Bridges in 1863, because of a population boom in the town. It became Penge West in 1923. The station building in the picture was heavily damaged by fire in 2005, but rebuilt. It was re-opened a year later. The down line platform buildings are all now gone and the platform can only be reached by a footbridge. (*Canon 750d*)

1 February 2020. No. 378 148 is caught between Penge West and Anerley stations on a stretch of line which is so straight; you can see one station from the other. Anerley station itself is very basic, having lost its station buildings and canopies and with a small ticket office now located on the down side. (*Canon 750d*)

7 February 2020. Re-liveried 378 136 heads towards Norwood Junction after leaving Anerley. The incline on the left carries the up line towards Crystal Palace from West Croydon and Norwood Junction. The bridge in the top right of the picture carries the Southern Line to Beckenham Junction over the Brighton Mainline, as well as a link to the down line over the Brighton Mainline, to curve and descend to the bottom right. (*Canon 750d*)

7 February 2020. Almost a full house in bright winter sunshine at Norwood Junction. A Southern 455 sits at Platform 6 with a Southern 377 at Platform 5. On Platform 3, a Thameslink 700 is about to leave, while on Platform 1, an Overground 378 has left. Norwood Junction technically doesn't have a Platform 2 as the Overground line is double sided, with doors only opening on the side of Platform 1. Network Rail has big plans to remodel this station with new platforms and footbridges (currently only a subway exists) as part of a wider scheme to improve lines between West and East Croydon and Norwood Junction. (*Canon 750d*)

7 February 2020. Not the station subway, but an important subway nonetheless. With Norwood Junction being so wide, this public subway links one side with the other under the station. The subway is important, as it was opened in 1912 as the world's first reinforced concrete underpass. Conceived by Borough engineer George Carter, it was built by none other than Robert McAlpine and sons. It even has its own 'unofficial' blue plaque on the entrance, located in front of the main station building. (*Canon 750d*)

1 February 2020. No. 378 140 arrives at bay Platform 1 at West Croydon. Before this station had its own dedicated platform for Overground services, trains would disembark passengers at Platform 4 and then run into a turnback beyond the station between the up and down lines. They would then return to the station to begin the journey back to East London. This is a practice now taken over by Southern services that terminate here. West Croydon is another station without a Platform 2, when Platform 3 was extended over it. (*Canon 750d*)

1 February 2020. A Croydon Tramlink CR4000 runs past the original station building in station road that is now a discount motor spares centre. However, the original entrance is still used as a side entrance onto Platform 4. West Croydon station is very well-connected, with tram and bus stops located right outside this entrance. No. 2550 is one of the original fleet of 24 CR4000 trams used on the Tramlink that are now being supplemented by brand new Variobahn trams. (*Canon 750d*)

7 February 2020. This is the 'new' 1930s entrance of West Croydon station on London Road, clearly showing its 1930s style. It has been smartened up in recent years, along with its neighbours, and has gained a coat of white paint over its bare concrete. It's also received more sympathetic and architecturally pleasing Overground branding on the front, with standout lettering in place of the more ubiquitous station name sign. This practice has been extended to its next-door neighbour, 'Roadrunners'. The tall building behind houses the Pinnacle apartments. (*Canon 750d*)

Chapter Four

Gospel Oak to Barking Line

The Gospel Oak to Barking Line, often known as the 'GOBLIN', or the T&H (Tottenham & Hampstead Junction Railway) to some railway diehards, has been the source of more grief than any other London Overground line in recent years, both to London Overground and to its passengers. The saga of its eventual electrification and rolling stock problems could fill a book on their own. And yet when the light at the end of the tunnel (no pun intended) was realised, it is a shining example of what effect investment (and patience) can do to a London railway. The transformation in passenger numbers alone would stand testimony to this. But the service as a whole has been transformed out of all recognition from the past as recent as the early 2000s. But it wasn't always so. In fact the original line the T&H in 1868, was a failure after just two years and closed, not even getting to Gospel Oak. It reopened under new owners and as the years went on, its western end destination changed no less than four times.

The line was progressively extended until it reached Barking at the end of the nineteenth century. At the time of writing, an extension is well under way to Barking Riverside. At the other end, having failed to reach Gospel Oak a first time, it was finally reached a second time before being abandoned and then reinstated again when the line terminated at a new bay platform built in 1981. This was because the former end of the route at Kentish Town was axed due to upgrade work outside St Pancras. Up until this point, like the North London Line, its passenger service had fought off closure under the Beeching Axe, but was so rundown that the line was literally unstaffed, its stations bereft of any comfort, and with a one train per hour frequency. It was more a freight line interrupted by a passenger service than the other way around. And not being electrified, that passenger service was having to make do with a plethora of ageing Diesel Multiple Units that went on far longer than they should have. But now we have the Gospel Oak to Barking line in its current form. Looking at it on a map you might think that it was an offshoot of the North London Line. Its 12 mile length takes about half an hour to travel its 12 stations. But at Gospel Oak *you do have to change trains.* Not so bad heading east but heading west entails something of a trek down to a deep underpass under the NLL and coming back up again.

Of course, the big problem that was associated with the GOBLIN was the fact that for the most part it wasn't electrified. It was always the odd man out in the Overground portfolio of lines. And as the years went on that became very problematic. The frequent freight services using it were in the main diesel hauled. And electric ones using the short electrified sections of the line only used it to gain access to other routes, especially through Tottenham. As mentioned, BR and NSE used a wide range of ageing DMUs on the route, although when Silverlink Metro took over, they used more modern class 150 DMUs. This was something of an improvement, alongside a better service and better stations. When London Overground took control, they replaced the 150s with sprightly class 172s. But they all had one thing in common. They were all only two coaches long. And with rising passenger numbers, even with a four trains per hour service, overcrowding became a big issue, especially in the peak. Because of the freight usage on the line it has a maximum capacity of eight trains per hour (tph) in each direction. Electrifying the whole route would mean more modern and longer trains and would bring the line into conformity with the rest of the Overground network. Electrically hauled freight could use it throughout as well. On a national railway network struggling to become electric in an environmental age, diesel power was going out of fashion. But electrifying a railway can be expensive, *very* expensive.

Addressing the issue in 2011, it should come as no surprise that the relevant parties, Department of Transport, TfL and Network Rail, couldn't agree on a plan of action. Cost estimates between them varied wildly. But by 2013, funding had finally been agreed and by late 2015, work began on electrifying the route, using a mix of part and full closures to end in early 2017. Track was lowered in some areas, and bridges rebuilt and raised in others, to make space for the overhead lines. Platforms were also lengthened where necessary for the new longer trains. By 2017 the line had reopened, but electrification work had still not been completed. Due to 'design and delivery' problems, it was not ready until 2018. Just in time for the delivery of the brand new 4-coach class 710 EMUs built by Bombardier to have been introduced on the route. Or so it was thought… Because of constant software problems with these new trains, their introduction date slipped – and kept on slipping. And it was then that a new problem, one that had been brewing for some time, emerged to complicate things even more. Some years before, it had been agreed to transfer the diesel-powered class 172s to West Midlands Trains to improve the services around Birmingham. The thinking back then was that by then the GOBLIN wouldn't be needing them. But with the class 710s still not ready it was beginning to look as if the route, now finally electrified, was going to be short of its electric trains. In the end West Midlands trains let the London Overground hang onto the class 172s as long as they could, but a solution had to be found. Ultimately it was a simple and expedient one, as it was found, after some testing, that Overground class 378s could be used in the interim. Taking a coach out of a normal 5-coach class 378 meant that they would fit the platforms on the line, especially at Gospel Oak, which is a tight squeeze even for a 4-coach train. So as the class 172s began to be transferred north the rest of the Overground network sacrificed one 378 (less one coach, stored at Willesden) from each of its other areas to keep the GOBLIN running. The last class 172 left Overground service in March 2019 and 378s took over completely to cover a reduced service. Technically speaking, while the service was now reduced, the capacity was still the same, as the shorter 378s were still twice as long as a class 172! (As a certain famous Meerkat would say, 'Simples'!) By mid-2019, software problems resolved, the brand new 710s began to enter service, and by late 2019 a full service of 4-coach trains was running every 15 minutes. As a 'thank you' for its passengers' patience, a free month's worth of travel on the line was paid for by Bombardier.

But just when the GOBLIN and its passengers were settling down to a new and improved normality something happened that would test their patience just that little bit longer. As mentioned, the route is a heavy freight artery around London, especially from the docks and industry at Tilbury. A temporary closure in 2008 for engineering work to improve bridges and track enabled it to carry more freight still. But early on 23 January 2020, a freight train derailed between Leyton Midland Road and Walthamstow Queens Road… and kept on going. In fact, it wasn't until it had run two and a half miles before something was noticed and it was brought to a standstill. But the damage had been done. Worse still, the most affected area was on a lot of the viaduct portion of the line as so much of the GOBLIN is. The damage was extraordinary. With a shuttle service running as far as South Tottenham, the entire line reopened after another month's closure. Working around the clock, Network Rail had replaced no less than 10,000 tons of ballast, along with more than 5,000 concrete and 900 wooden sleepers and 39 stretches of rail. Bridge timbers had to be repaired as well, many of them custom made. After all this we can only hope that the GOBLIN is trouble free for some time to come…

26 June 2020. Gospel Oak Station entrance sits on Gordon House Road in the London Borough of Camden. The original station that opened here in 1860 was named Kentish Town until 1867 when it was renamed Gospel Oak. A new and more appropriately sited Kentish Town station was then opened nearer to Kentish Town. The North London line tracks cross the bridge on the right. It only became a passenger interchange in 1981 when the passenger line to Kentish Town was amended to start and finish at this station instead. (*Canon 750d*)

1 February 2019. After a dusting of snow, 172 008 sits in the bay platform at Gospel Oak, ticking over its diesel engine on a bitterly cold Friday afternoon. No. 66 562 rolls past, having just taken its Freightliner from the North London Line onto the Gospel Oak to Barking line over Gospel Oak Junction in the background. Despite the route now being electrified, these DMUs would soldier on for a few more months yet. (*Canon 750d*)

15 February 2019. The interior of 172 001 while waiting at Gospel Oak. The 2+2 seating of these 2-car 172/0 'Turbostars' enables a seating capacity of 124 people. When London Overground took over the Gospel Oak to Barking line from Silverlink Metro in 2007, it dispensed with their class 150 DMUs after a short while and ordered eight of these 172s instead. They soldiered on until March 2019, with 172 001 being one of the last to be transferred to East Midlands Trains. (*Canon 750d*)

15 April 2019. A brand new Bombardier 710 (263) 'Aventra' runs off the North London Line onto the Gospel Oak to Barking Line past the empty bay platform at Gospel Oak for an afternoon run of testing and driver training. The 710 is from the 'Aventra' family of Electric Multiple Units that all look very similar. When they finally entered service, they would be a quantum leap from the Class 172 DMUs that GOBLIN passengers would have been used to in the past, being twice as long, electric, and have such things as air conditioning, onboard displays and WiFi! (*Fuji X-S1*)

2 August 2019. The interior of a class 710 'Aventra' at Gospel Oak looking down towards the rearmost cab. In common with the Overground class 378s, the seating is all longitudinal, with some seats being flip up/down to make extra space for bikes and buggies. A standard 4-car has seating capacity for 189 people. While this doesn't sound like a huge increase over the half as long 172s they were replacing, the big difference was in the standing room at 489 people! (*Fuji X-S1*)

10 January 2020. No. 710 259 is just about to disappear under the covered way that the Acland Burghley School, Youth Centre and Camden Fencing Club now sits upon. On the extreme left can just be seen the tunnel mouth of the route to the Midland Mainline, when the line terminated at Kentish Town. It's now used for freight. In the distance can be seen another class 710 on its way to Gospel Oak, where the former Highgate Road High Level station could also have been found until it closed in 1915. (*Canon 750d*)

1 February 2019. No. 172 007 comes past the 'portacabin' signal box at Upper Holloway in the snow. This rather rudimentary signal box of BR design opened in 1985 and replaced two earlier Midland Railway signal boxes called Upper Holloway and Junction Road Junction. The lines branching off to the left are all that's left of Tufnell Park Goods depot which finally closed in 1968. Now barely a couple of sidings left, these are used as a freight loop, for engineering trains and latterly for reversing new class 710s on test and driver training. (*Canon 750d*)

17 April 2019. Europhoenix/Rail Operations Group 37 611 *Pegasus* comes though Upper Holloway station, hot on the heels of a class 710 on testing and driver training. With software problems plaguing the introduction of the 710s into public service, these class 37 diesel locomotives play 'stalking horse' to the new units, ready to rescue them if they choose to 'sit down' on the job. This is chiefly possible because these class 37s are fitted with a Dellner coupler, making them compatible with any other train so fitted, including the new 710s. (*Canon 750d*)

23 May 2019. This was something of a red-letter day on the GOBLIN. As we see 710 269 on the first official day of service for these new trains. Only two units would be operating initially, with the remaining six running by August 2019 meaning a full service of one train every 15 minutes would be operated over the route. (*Fuji X-S1*)

10 January 2020. Crouch Hill station bathed in winter afternoon sunlight. It was always a very simple affair since its opening in 1868, and it is even more simple now, as the reader can see. However, upon visiting, the author found that someone had manufactured a 'Minion' from some car tyres and tubing on the embankment behind Platform 2! (*Canon 750d*)

2 August 2019. No. 710 265 runs into Harringay Green Lanes Station from the direction of Barking. Of note in this photo, on either side of the track are the original concrete piles of the earlier very long platforms here. Extra-long ones were provided to cope with the crowds going to and from Harringay Stadium. They were cut back in 2003 due to subsidence six years after the stadium closed, and these days they are long enough for the 4-car class 710s seen in the picture. (*Fuji X-S1*)

1 February 2019. A weather-worn 172 001 passes South Tottenham Signal Box at South Tottenham Station, between cold and wet snow showers. South Tottenham Signal Box is a former Great Eastern box and was built in 1894. The platforms here, in common with many others on the route, had been shortened before being extended again. The most recent extension on the up platform can be seen where the waiting shelter sits directly in front of the signal box. (*Canon 750d*)

1 February 2019. Looking the other way back towards Gospel Oak, we can see the undulating nature of the route here, as 172 004 has just climbed the short incline into South Tottenham Station and is now passing over the bridge that crosses the road below. Beneath the last bogie of the second coach can just be seen the beginning of the points of the Seven Sisters Curve, linking the route to the Enfield Town/Cheshunt Lea Valley Line. (*Canon 750d*)

17 April 2019. No. 710 269 approaches South Tottenham over South Tottenham East Junction on a test and driver training run. The train indicator says 'Not in Service' and printed signs could also be found stuck up in the windows of the doors, warning passengers not to try and board the train. While the train stopped for a few brief minutes in the station, several passengers tried to do just that! The tracks going straight on provide a link to the Greater Anglia Line to Hertford East and Stansted Airport. (*Canon 750d*)

2 August 2019. Freightliner 66 607 rolls across the rebuilt elevated section with a cement train that carries the line across the River Lea and the beginning of the Walthamstow Wetlands. No. 66 607 was among a batch of 19 class 66s ordered by Freightliner, which had reduced gearing to help enable them to cope better with heavy oil, aggregate, and as you can see here, cement trains. (*Fuji X-S1*)

2 August 2019. The Marine Engine Pump House at Walthamstow Wetlands Centre stands alongside the Gospel Oak to Barking route between South Tottenham and Blackhorse Road stations. Constructed in 1894, and previously known as the Ferry Lane Pumping Station, it pumped water through the reservoirs along with the Coppermill Pump House the other side of the Wetlands. It's now been restored with a new Chimney that houses bird boxes, and is now the home to the Engine House Café and the Wetlands education centre. An upstairs outside terrace gives good views over the surrounding area. (*Fuji X-S1*)

2 August 2019. In a break of sunshine, 710 264 comes past the Walthamstow Marine Engine Pump House along the elevated section over the River Lea. In the background can be seen new apartments and housing being built at Blackhorse Road. By this time, the whole fleet of class 710s had been rolled out on the Gospel Oak to Barking Line after a very intensive period of driver training and testing. (*Fuji X-S1*)

2 August 2019. Having crossed the causeway across Walthamstow Wetlands and reservoirs, 710 264 rolls into Blackhorse Road Station, with the new Blackhorse Mills apartment complex being built in the background. The current station here was re-sited in 1981 after having previously been a little further east on the other side of Blackhorse Road Bridge. (*Fuji X-S1*)

2 August 2019. The current Blackhorse Road Station opened in 1981, a little further west from the original station that opened in 1894, which was located the other side of the main road bridge that crosses the line. This was done so that the London Underground station beneath, serving the Victoria Line, could have a seamless interchange with the national rail station above. Note that the station carries both the roundels of London Underground and London Overground. (*Fuji X-S1*)

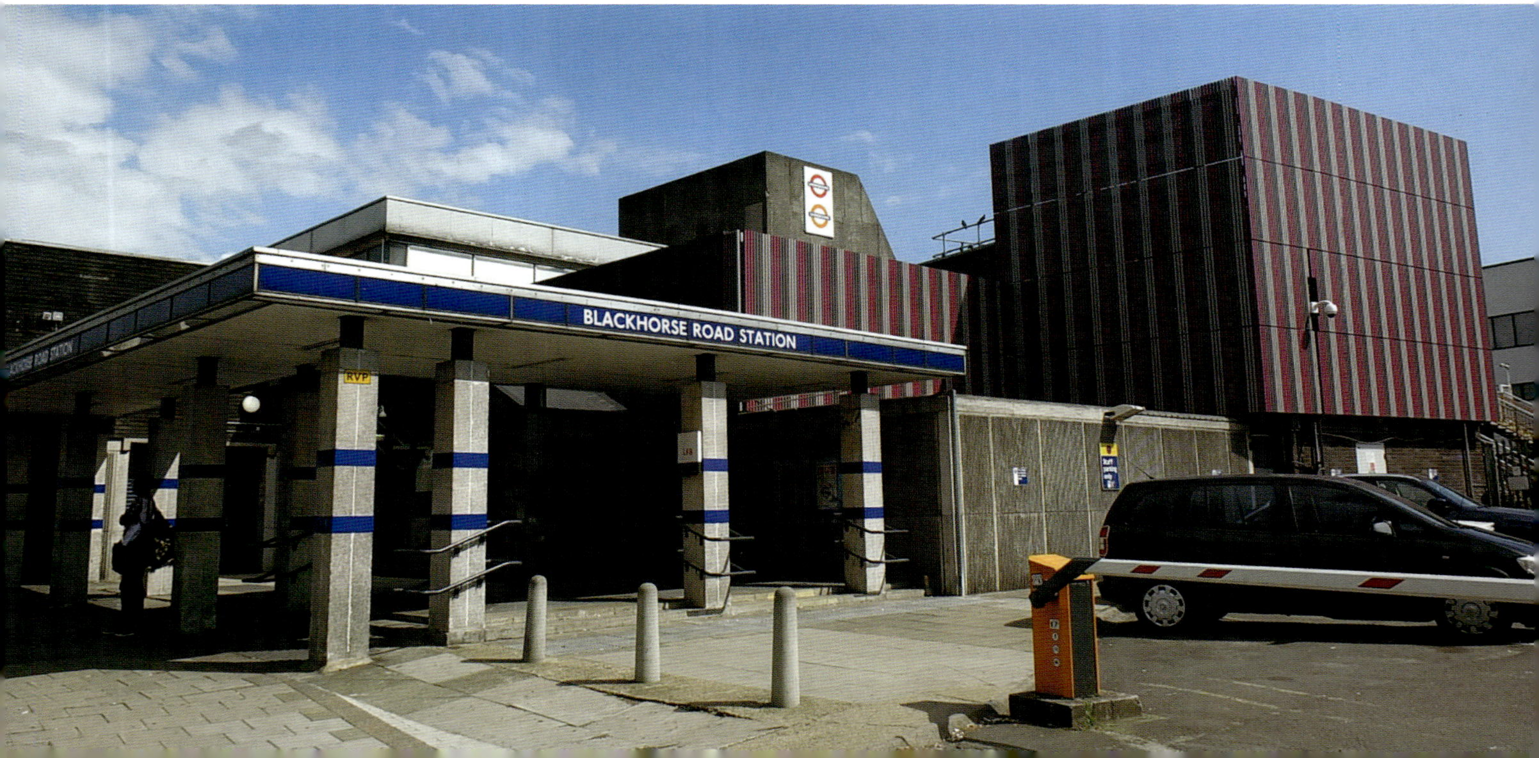

10 January 2020. With London Overground's drive to make as many of their stations as accessible as possible, and where lifts have either not been practicable because of cost or other reasons, they have installed long ramps to reach platform level. These are a notable feature of many of the stations on the Gospel Oak to Barking route; and one of the best examples is here at Walthamstow Queens Road. With very little in the way of any station buildings, these ramps are a standout feature. (*Canon 750d*)

10 January 2020. No. 710 259 is about to arrive at Walthamstow Queens Road after travelling under Shrubland Road Bridge. Beyond that is a substantial amount of bracing that covers the track to reinforce the retaining walls of the cutting here. Walthamstow Central Station, on London Underground's Victoria Line and the London Overground line to Chingford, is a 300-yard walk from this station up Ray Dudley Way, named after a local campaigner who fought to get the link built. (*Canon 750d*)

15 February 2019. The eastern end of the Gospel Oak to Barking line is very much elevated on a viaduct, and nowhere is this illustrated better than at Leyton Midland Road Station. Here we see 172 007 approach the station across the curved arch viaduct in some winter sunshine. It's also worth bearing in mind that when the route was finally electrified between 2015 and 2018, installing the overhead catenary was a major challenge on these stretches, with many supports having to be fixed directly onto the side of the viaducts in question. (*Canon 750d*)

15 February 2019. A waiting passenger looks on as the bright red DB Schenker 90 028, *Sir William McAlpine*, hurries through Leyton Midland Road with a car train in tow, probably from the Ford plant at Dagenham. Electrifying the route throughout means more flexible working by the freight operators using the Gospel Oak to Barking Line, who no longer have to depend solely on diesel haulage. (*Canon 750d*)

23 May 2019. No. 378 216 arrives at Leyton Midland Road heading for Gospel Oak, during the rolling stock shortage on the Gospel Oak to Barking Line in the first half of 2019. With the 172s now all having gone north to West Midlands Trains, a few 5-car 378s were shorn of a carriage to fit platform lengths on the route, and pressed into a half-hourly service instead of the usual four trains per hour. While not as frequent, at least passengers had a foretaste of what was to come with the 4-car 710s when they entered service! (*Fuji X-S1*)

15 February 2019. No. 172 001 arrives at Leyton Midland Road heading for Gospel Oak as 172 005 has just departed, heading for Barking. No. 172 001, along with 004 and 007, would be one of the last three class 172s to depart from London Overground to transfer to West Midlands Trains one month later; so getting a shot of two Overground 172s together so 'late in the day' was a nice catch. (*Canon 750d*)

25 June 2020. No. 710 271 curves into Leytonstone High Road on one of the hottest days of 2020. The passengers on board won't be feeling it, though, because the class 710s have some of the best air-conditioning that the author has ever experienced on a train! Leytonstone High Road was opened simply as Leytonstone in 1894 and didn't get its current name until 1949. The station went through a period of neglect after the war robbed it of many of its features. These days, bus stop-type shelters suffice on bare platforms reached from stairs to street level, as seen in the picture. (*Canon 750d*)

2 March 2019. No. 378 232 crosses the bridge over the A114/Woodford Road into Wanstead Park station at about 4pm in the afternoon. No. 378 232 was the first 'guinea pig' 378 to be used on the GOBLIN and would be joined later by 206 and 209. Passenger services have used an eclectic mix of rolling stock on the route in its history. Under BR and Network Southeast, types used included class 104, 105 and 117 DMUs. Under Silverlink Metro, class 150 DMUs were used before the Overground 172 DMUs gave way to class 378 and finally the 710 EMUs! (*Fuji X-S1*)

25 June 2020. Many of the stations on the Gospel Oak to Barking Line, especially in the latter half, are situated on viaducts. Most if not all had substantial platform and station buildings upon opening, until the war and even after. But this picture, taken at Wanstead Park, illustrates the norm on so many stations on the route now. A staircase descends from each platform either side of the viaduct to ticket barriers and facilities under or at the base of an arch. A small booth or prefab often serves as a small office for staff. (*Canon 750d*)

2 March 2019. Coming in the opposite direction from the previous photo is 378 209. The whole of Wanstead Park station has been built on a curve and like many of the Overground Stations, this end of the line is elevated and built on viaducts. The zoom effect of the camera lens, however, has increased the apparent curvature of the approach. (*Fuji X-S1*)

26 June 2020. No. 710 264 comes into Woodgrange Park Station, the penultimate stop before the end of the line at Barking. Formerly on the London Tilbury & Southend Line between Liverpool Street and Barking, it received electrification many years before the rest of the route to Gospel Oak. Woodgrange Park Junction, where the line diverges to Liverpool Street, can be seen beyond the road bridge. The imposing archway above the train is all that's left of the street level buildings. Its twin, for the up line platform, is out of shot to the left. (*Canon 750d*)

2 March 2019. No. 172 004 approaches Barking at the end of its journey. On my wanderings around the area, I was struck by just how fenced and caged in the railways around Barking station were. The footbridge at the top of the picture perfectly illustrates this and has sadly become the norm across Britain's railway network. The plethora of overhead catenary and supporting masts didn't help much, either. However, I was able to find this vantage point after much searching. (*Canon 750d*)

2 March 2019. No. 373 232 leaves Barking Station, bound for Gospel Oak at the other end of the line. It's departing from Platform 1, currently dedicated to Overground services, though Platform 7 is sometimes used. A London Underground District Line S-stock train sits at Platform 2, about to continue on to Upminster, while another has terminated in the bay Platform 3. (*Canon 750d*)

25 June 2020. No. 710 254 sits at Platform 7, Barking Station, minutes from returning back to Gospel Oak. Overground Services more often than not use the bay Platform 1, but sometimes also use Platform 7 when a problem arises, which means a platform change. However, when the extension to Barking Riverside opens in 2022, this platform will become the normal one for Overground services at Barking. (*Canon 750d*)

Chapter Five

Lea Valley Lines

London Liverpool Street to Enfield Town and Cheshunt

The Lea Valley lines out of Liverpool Street were the most recent to be added to London Overground's portfolio in 2015. So-called because they run along the lower Lea Valley of the river Lea in eastern greater London. They were run by a mixture of Eastern Railway companies until absorbed into the Great Eastern Railway (GER) in 1862. They then came under the Eastern Region of BR in 1948 before becoming part of the West Anglia subdivision of British Railways Network Southeast in 1982. Upon privatisation in 1997, the routes were run by a succession of franchises with the word 'Anglia' in the title until last owned by Abellio Greater Anglia as part of the Greater Anglia franchise. The routes were electrified to the 25kv AC overhead system in the 1960s.

Beginning at Liverpool Street in East London, the line passes under the East London Line before climbing up a substantial gradient to Bethnal Green. It then continues onwards to the major station at Hackney Downs, crossing over the North London Line. Just after Hackney Downs, the line to Enfield Town and Cheshunt curves away to the left while the Chingford Branch curves right. Cheshunt is at such a distance of 14 miles, however, that it can be found in Zone 8 on TfL's zone system. The only other London Overground station further than this is Watford Junction, just beyond Zone 9. Enfield Town and Chingford both lie just over 10 miles from Liverpool Street. Between Edmonton Green and Cheshunt the line was often referred to as the Southbury or Churchbury Loop. A long since closed branch from Edmonton Green to Angel Road on the former Great Eastern Line (now Greater Anglia) to Cheshunt via Angel Road, created this loop. The Southbury/Churchbury Loop was never popular, being so rural, and unable to compete with the tram it closed to passenger workings between 1909 and 1960. Electrification of the Lea Valley lines in the 60s gave it a new lease of life and passenger services were reintroduced.

Many of the stations are built on viaducts above street level and many stations have retained their late 1800s GER style and architecture in some form or another. One exception, though, is the rebuilding of the station at White Hart Lane, which was undertaken when Tottenham FC rebuilt their stadium in 2017–19. To cope with increased match day crowds the nearby station was greatly expanded and rebuilt to a modern style, opening in 2019. At the time of writing, rolling stock is mostly comprised of ageing 4-car class 315 and 317 EMUs in a smart Overground livery. But it wasn't' uncommon to also find TfL Rail liveried class 315s running on these lines as well. This is because some had been transferred from the TfL Rail run Liverpool Street to Shenfield line as new class 345s were introduced on this route in preparation for it becoming the eastern end of

'Crossrail'. Brand new class 710 EMUs (externally similar to the 345s), working in multiple (which caused some early software problems) have just been introduced on the Lea Valley Lines, and by the time this book is published, will have taken over. Most services run every half an hour, though up to Hackney Downs train frequency is double that as services to Enfield Town and Cheshunt both use this stretch. Services to Chingford tend to run fast from Liverpool Street to Hackney Downs.

29 November 2019. Just under a month to go before Christmas, and Liverpool Street Station is crowded as usual in the evening rush hour. Designed by the Great Eastern Engineer Edward Wilson, it opened in 1874 as the Great Eastern's London Railway terminus; and is located in the Bishopsgate area of the City of London. It was expanded at the end of the eighteenth century, but by the 1970s, its limitations were showing again, so this station and the station next door, Broad Street, were up for demolition and redevelopment. However, a successful campaign led by the poet John Betjeman (who was also instrumental in saving St Pancras Station) saved it. Broad Street Station was sacrificed for the Broadgate development instead, while Liverpool Street was kept, but underwent its own limited redevelopment which was completed in 1991. This gives us the station we see today. (*Canon 750d*)

29 November 2019. London Overground 317 710, still bearing its remembrance poppy motif, waits at Platform 1, about to leave for Cheshunt, while a class 315 sits alongside in the distance. The station serves Greater Anglia, Stansted Express, TfL Rail and London Overground services, with the latter leaving from Platforms 1, 2 and 7. As can be seen, the rolling stock on the Lea Valley Lines was far older than the rest of the Overground Network. They used a mixture of ageing class 315 and 317 AC electric multiple units inherited from Greater Anglia, who in turn inherited them from British Rail, who introduced them in the 1980s. (*Canon 750d*)

25 May 2019. No. 315 808 climbs the steep ascent out of Liverpool Street Station into the first stop on the route, Bethnal Green. The exit from Liverpool Street Station, some of which is under the Broadgate development, and mostly in a cutting, takes on an almost subterranean feel; and in steam days would have been even worse, with steam locomotives working hard on the 1 in 65 climb out. The electrification of the Lea Valley lines was completed by 1960, making things a lot easier (and cleaner!). (*Fuji X-S1*)

25 May 2019. No. 315 808 has just arrived at Bethnal Green, while 315 802 is approaching, bound for Liverpool Street. The 315 units were built at the BREL (British Railways Engineering Ltd) works at York and introduced onto Britain's Railways from 1980/81, so are now 40 years old. Like all the Overground stations from Liverpool Street to Hackney Downs, Bethnal Green Station is situated on a viaduct and lacks any platform buildings or even a shelter. People tend to use the exits and entrances on the stairs to ground level for shelter instead. (*Fuji X-S1*)

25 May 2019. No. 315 801 takes the sharp curve into Bethnal Green Station that aligns the Lea Valley fast and slow lines, with the Great Eastern Main Line out of shot on the right. This unit is the first of the class from a batch of 19 operated by London Overground, though they are slowly being phased out for scrapping in 2020/21. They were the last in a line of BR standard Electric Multiple Units built to a 1972 design, the rest being classes 313, 314, 501 and 502. The 313s are dual voltage, whereas the 314s and 315s can only be used on the 25kv AC overhead electrification. The 501s and 502s work the third rail Merseyrail network. (*Fuji X-S1*)

15 June 2020. Cambridge Heath Station has a more modern frontage than most with a design dating from the mid-1980s, after the original station building burnt down in a fire in 1984, briefly closing the station. It's also in keeping with the other street level buildings that are based within the arches of the viaduct. The almost bus stop-like design of its street sign is noticeable. (*Canon 750d*)

15 June 2020. With its lifespan now measured in days if not weeks, 315 815 comes into Cambridge Heath Station, bound for Liverpool Street. By the time this photo had been taken, the class 317s had all but gone from London Overground's inventory and the new class 710s, working in multiple as two 4-cars, were fast taking over. The platform 'buildings' seen in the picture are all that is left at platform level, with the canopies and everything else long since gone. (*Canon 750d*)

25 May 2019. The street level buildings of London Fields Station are incorporated into the arches beneath the tracks above. Opened along with Cambridge Heath in 1872, it underwent some alteration when the route along here changed from two tracks to four, the last two now being the fast lines. However, in 1981, the station here was badly damaged by fire that effectively closed it until a rebuilding and refurbishment reopened it in 1986. (*Fuji X-S1*)

25 May 2019. No. 315 814 arrives at Platform 1 at London Fields Station. The fire of 1981 effectively led to the demolition of all the buildings on the down platform, but upon the refurbishment of the station, those of the up platform were swept away as well. This once again gives a station devoid of any shelter except for the entrance/exits on the stairwell to ground level. The tower in the background is the 16-storey Vanguard House, a residential tower block built in 2003/2004. (*Fuji X-S1*)

20 April 2019. A good overall view of Hackney Downs Station, seen from the London end of Platform 4. Platforms 4 & 3 serve trains to and from Enfield Town and Cheshunt, while Platforms 2 & 1 (3 & 2 being the island platform) serve trains to and from Chingford. Greater Anglia trains also call here twice an hour to and from Hertford East. Adding to that the non-stopping Greater Anglia and Stansted Express services to and from Stansted Airport make Hackney Downs a very busy station. (*Fuji X-S1*)

24 May 2019. TfL Rail liveried 315 858 stands on Platform 3 at Hackney Downs. At first glance, it may seem that this unit is an interloper from the Liverpool Street to Shenfield TfL Rail line, but a closer inspection will reveal an orange London Overground roundel applied over the dark blue TfL Rail one on the body side. As TfL Rail took delivery of their new class 745 'Aventra's' on the Liverpool Street to Shenfield service, London Overground took delivery of the cast-off 315s from the route to boost their own services and to replace the older 315s in their own fleet. (*Fuji X-S1*)

20 April 2019. No. 317 710, seen earlier in the book at Liverpool Street, arrives at Hackney Downs from Cheshunt. The London Overground livery suits the class 315s and 317s very well, if it's kept clean! The class 317 units have had differing front end profiles over the years depending on what mark they are. The London Overground 317/7s were formally 317/1s that Greater Anglia refurbished with a slightly different cab roof profile and headlight clusters. The interiors have been redone as well. (*Fuji X-S1*)

15 June 2020. Brand new class 710 'Aventras' built by Bombardier began to run in service on the Lea Valley Lines at the start of March 2020, replacing the class 317 units on the Liverpool Street to Cheshunt services. In time, they replaced the 315 units as well. Here we see 710 121 leading another 4-car unit coupled on behind into Rectory Road. (*Canon 750d*)

10 October 2019. No. 317 890, a 317 in the 8 series, is another refurbished series 1 unit, but without the new look front end, presenting an earlier, more boxy style instead. Here it arrives at Stoke Newington Station which is situated in a brick-lined cutting with road bridges at either end that give it a rather confined feel. The canopy on the down platform behind the train is a shadow of the former platform canopies that used to line the tracks here. All were dismantled and taken away in the mid-70s, along with the stairway roofing as well. (*Canon 750d*)

10 October 2019. Taken from the curving up platform, 317 817 is framed in the arch of the road bridge carrying the main station building above, as well as being the junction for Manor Road, Belfast Road and the A10. In the distance on the left, where the track curves away, was Stoke Newington Goods Depot of a couple of sidings and a loop. This closed in 1964 and is now a small local park called Allens Gardens. (*Canon 750d*)

3 October 2019. No. 315 858, another former TfL Rail 315 unit in London Overground service, rounds the curve into Stamford Hill station. During June 2020, it wasn't uncommon to see both former TfL Rail and London Overground 315s running together to make eight cars on some services, after the 317 units had all been withdrawn and class 710s were being brought into service. Depending on mileage and condition, some former TfL Rail 315s were outlasting their London Overground brethren. (*Fuji X-S1*)

25 June 2020. Looking in the opposite direction at Stamford Hill, we see the substantial street level buildings from the rear, leading down to the platforms. All the windows have now been bricked up, bar one on the rebuilt section, but this is being supported by external bracing on the embankment on the far left. The more modern staircases take up space that was once filled by platform canopies. Interestingly, the station is in two boroughs, with the main buildings in the picture being in Hackney and the platforms lying in Haringey! (*Canon 750d*)

15 June 2020. No. 710 119, with 710 120 on the rear, runs into Seven Sisters Station bound for Cheshunt. This station is a shadow of its former self, now sharing a narrow street level entrance with the London Underground Victoria Line below. Up until the mid-60s, it was a large junction station serving the Palace Gates Branch, which closed to passengers in 1963 and to freight two years later. Services would join from South Tottenham below, on the Seven Sisters cord branching off left in the background, or run from Liverpool Street. The branch itself, and its platforms, would leave just where the platforms have been extended on the right, now the site of Brunswick Road open space behind the present station. (*Canon 750d*)

3 October 2019. Bruce Grove Station opened in 1872 and is seen from street level. The painting of the station's name on the bridges, that are a common sight on the viaduct sections of the route, isn't a new thing. The Great Eastern Railway saw them as perfect advertising space and would plaster them with the station's name, notices and adverts to other destinations. (*Fuji X-S1*)

3 October 2019. Bruce Grove Station is built on something of a curve next to the A10 main road. But perhaps the most pleasing thing about it is the fact that, at platform level at least, it hasn't much changed. The canopy on the up platform has remained, under which we see 317 729 with its modified front end arriving at the down platform. This platform lost its canopy and buildings in 1979 and yet a new canopy, like the original, was then later erected, giving a much smarter appearance to the station. (*Fuji X-S1*)

10 October 2019. As mentioned elsewhere in this book, London Overground doesn't have First Class on its trains. However, while its 317/7 units were running on its network, they kept the first-class compartments inherited from their Greater Anglia days and just branded them as standard class instead! And what luxury! In an age where railway seating has become akin to sitting on an ironing board, such comfort as this on London's railways is now almost a thing of the past. (*Canon 750d*)

3 October 2019. No. 315 814 runs into White Hart Lane Station past the old station building, heading for Liverpool Street. The station opened in July 1872, but suffered bad fire damage in 1977, which was subsequently repaired. The canopies have been modified in the spirit of the original ones. Workmen can be seen doing work on the old building shortly before a new building, further down the platform, was opened, in conjunction with a new higher capacity stadium for Tottenham Hotspur Football Club, just a stone's throw away. (*Fuji X-S1*)

29 November 2019. The new White Hart Lane Station building, seen during its first days of opening. When Tottenham Hotspur Football Club had their stadium rebuilt just yards away, the increased capacity saw a new station being built for bigger crowds. A new similar building can also be found adjoining the opposite platform. Both have multiple entrances and exits and plentiful provision of platform access. The old station building can still be seen at the end for a comparison. (*Canon 750d*)

25 June 2020. No. 315 808 arrives at Silver Street, working in multiple with another 315 on the rear. As the class 710s began to take over from 317s and 315s, it seemed that surviving 315s were being worked in multiples as eight cars before retirement. The station reputedly takes its name from the fact that many silver smiths worked in the area in ancient times. It's also not far from either the previous station, White Hart Lane, 0.8 miles away, or the next station, Edmonton Green, at 0.6 miles away. (*Fuji X-S1*)

24 May 2019. The author had a knack of capturing 317 710 on camera for pictures in this book and here it is again, leading another 317 coupled on behind. But this shot also shows to good effect the undulating route between Silver Street, visible in the far distance through the midday heat haze, and Edmonton Green Station where this unit is about to arrive. (*Fuji X-S1*)

25 June 2020. Edmonton Green Station as seen from street level. Originally named Edmonton and then Lower Edmonton, it became Edmonton Green in 1992, shortly after the flat building bearing the station name was added. The lift shafts to make the station completely accessible (another one is located the other side) are a more recent addition still. If nothing else, this station is very colourful! (*Canon 750d*)

24 May 2019. A fine study of 315 808 returning from Enfield Town on the curve into Edmonton Green Station. Behind the train once ran the 1849 Eastern Counties branch line from Angel Road, which joined this line further on at Edmonton Junction. It also had a station off to the right called Lower Edmonton Low Level, closing to passengers in 1939. It was briefly reopened as a diversionary route before closing for good in 1964. No trace of it survives today, being buried under the Edmonton Green Shopping Centre. (*Fuji X-S1*)

10 October 2019. We've now curved off onto the Enfield Town branch and are at Bush Hill Park Station. It had its original 1880s main station building on the down side, opening out onto a nice parade of shops with a village feel to it. This, however, is the much simpler building on the up side built mid-1890s. When the main down side building succumbed to fire in 1981 and was replaced with a brick hut, this upside building then became the main entrance. It has a nice platform canopy the other side. (*Canon 750d*)

10 October 2019. No. 315 810 approaches Bush Hill Park Station, having just crossed over Lincoln Road Level Crossing. In the distance, the line curves around to terminate at Enfield Town. The 315s often run as four cars, while the 317s often run as eight cars on the longer Cheshunt route. (*Canon 750d*)

19 October 2019. There aren't many manned level crossings on the London railway network these days, but Lincoln Road Level Crossing is one of them. Located on the approach to Enfield Town, the crossing keeper locks and unlocks the pedestrian gates via a lever on a warning of an approaching train. Road traffic is no longer allowed at the crossing and though a footbridge has often been considered, the area is very built up. So for now this railway anachronism is staying. Here, 317 890 is about to pass the permanently locked road gates on the crossing. (*Canon 750d*)

24 May 2019. No. 315 802, one of the last two Overground 315s to be retired in Oct 2020, at Platform 2, Enfield Town Station, at the end of the line on the Enfield Town branch. This station has three platforms, but only Platform 2 is in regular operation for the one train every half an hour back into Liverpool Street. The extensive goods yards and engine shed have all gone, but a small ground frame and levers still exist for a set of run round points at the station end. One can only guess when they were last used! (*Fuji X-S1*)

29 November 2019. Now back on the line to Cheshunt, Southbury is the first station we come to. Opened as Churchbury by the Great Eastern Railway in 1891, the station survived two closures in 1909 and 1919. It continues to be a true survivor, all but untouched by the past 130 years of progress. But one can only wonder why the building next door was allowed to be built without some kind of aesthetic effort being made to blend with its neighbour! The station was renamed Southbury with the beginning of the electric services in 1960. (*Canon 750d*)

29 November 2019. Southbury Station seen from platform level in as good a condition as the street view. This part of the route, also known as the Southbury/Churchbury Loop, lost its passenger services after 1910; and was used for freight or as a diversionary route until electrification in 1960 brought back the passenger services. The link of this line to the Greater Anglia (formally Great Eastern) line at Cheshunt, and the former branch to Angel Road on the same line at Edmonton Green, made up the loop. (*Canon 750d*)

29 November 2019. With less than a month to go until Christmas, the afternoon winter sun highlights the tracks and what leaves are left on the trees as 315 802 approaches the interestingly named Turkey Street Station. Opened as Forty Hill in 1861, it had a name change like Southbury in 1960, when passenger services resumed over the route. The current name is taken from the Turkey Brook, a little stream that runs under the bridge the train is about to cross. All station buildings have gone and now a small glass and metal entrance suffices at street level. (*Canon 750d*)

15 June 2020. The view at Theobalds Grove between 710 119 and 710 120 coupled together to make an 8-car train. Only at one other place on the London Overground network does the passenger exceed the limits of Zone 6 on the London Zonal Travel Map: on the Watford DC lines at Carpenders Park towards Watford Junction. (*Canon 750d*)

20 June 2020. Nos. 710 120 and 119 photographed again on their return journey from Cheshunt. The service on this upper reach of the Lea Valley London Overground line is one train every half an hour; and with the end of the line at the next stop, if a down service is cancelled, anyone waiting for an up train has a long wait ahead of them. (*Canon 750d*)

29 November 2019. The end of the line at Cheshunt Station out in the wilds of Zone 8. All London Overground services terminate in the single line bay platform on the left, with the Greater Anglia Line between London Liverpool Street and Hertford East being on the right. The lines, however, are connected at Cheshunt Junction. (*Canon 750d*)

29 November 2019. The large original Great Eastern station building of 1891 that stood here was sadly demolished so the bay platform could be extended to accommodate 8-coach trains. Its replacement, seen here, is a much smaller metal and glass construction, not unlike that of Turkey Street. Behind the station is Windmill Lane level crossing and a non-station footbridge. (*Canon 750d*)

Chapter Six

Lea Valley Lines

Liverpool Street to Chingford

20 April 2019. Morning sunlight shines in through the roof of Liverpool Street Station as 315 814 sits at Platform 7, waiting to leave for its journey to Chingford. A Greater Anglia class 350 'Desiro' waits alongside, on a service to Ipswich. Liverpool Street Station has 18 platforms in total and is one of the largest termini in London. With the station split into two basic halves, East and West, the Lea Valley Lines operate from the western half alongside the Greater Anglia services to Hertford East. (*Fuji X-S1*)

20 April 2019. The interior of a London Overground class 315 Electric Multiple Unit, very lightly loaded on a late morning run to Chingford. The seating is the standard 3+2, with the seats in the London Overground moquette of orange and two-tone brown. Looking quite dated by today's modern standards, at least the seats are latitudinal as opposed to running longitudinal, as is the norm on the class 378s and new class 710s. (*Fuji X-S1*)

25 May 2019. In bright sunshine, 315 809 flies past Cambridge Heath on the fast lines. Most Chingford services run fast from Liverpool Street to Hackney Downs, while services to Enfield Town and Cheshunt tend to stop at all stations. Note that this unit is a 315 with a different headlight design to most, being of different sizes and inclined, as opposed a standard size and horizontal design. (*Fuji X-S1*)

24 May 2019. Beautifully lit by the afternoon sun, 315 802, the second of the class, is seen from the London end of Platform 4 on the approach to Hackney Downs Station, about to cross over Hackney Downs South Junction. Chingford services usually run every 15 minutes from Liverpool Street fast to Hackney Downs. The only service better than this at present is the TfL rail service to Shenfield, which will become part of Crossrail when it opens. This runs every 10 minutes. (*Fuji X-S1*)

15 June 2020 An Overground class 710 creeps into Hackney Downs heading to Liverpool Street behind the former BR Signal Box. This box, with its very prominent sun-shade, opened in 1960 and replaced the Hackney Downs Junction signal box that was located in the background. When the signalling was then completed by the Liverpool Street Signalling Control Centre in 2001, it was taken out of use. But it still stands today. (*Canon 750d*)

20 April 2019. On what looks like a summer's afternoon, 315 815 stands at Platform 1 at Hackney Downs, having arrived from Chingford, while another unit has just departed Platform 2 in the background. The people walking along the platform, far right, are making their way to the Hackney Central Overground station via the long covered bi-level walkway that links the two, situated at the end of this platform. (*Fuji X-S1*)

20 April 2019. Clapton Station is in a lined cutting crossed by bridges above, not unlike Stoke Newington on the Enfield Town/Cheshunt branch. The bridge in the background carries the Upper Clapton Road/A107, while the bridge above in the picture carries Southwold Road. No. 315 804 is caught in the sunlight between the two as a solitary would-be passenger looks on. The canopy on the upside platform is amazingly the original one dating from the 1870s, while the one on the down side was removed in the 1970s. (*Fuji X-S1*)

20 April 2019. Where is everyone?! A truly desolate St James Street Station on a hot Saturday afternoon, although it sees a little over 1.1 million passengers a year. Two brick platform shelters covering the stairs to ground level, behind the photographer, are the only platform shelter here, so passengers are a bit hard hit come rain or hot sunshine. The station opened in 1870 and, after a short while, was provided with entrances at either end of the platforms. However, those at the eastern end, little used, were finally closed and demolished in 1967. (*Fuji X-S1*)

20 April 2019 Walthamstow Central Station is a major interchange with the London Underground Victoria Line and local bus routes, all of which can be found off the platform entrance to the left. On the right, above 315 802, just arriving, is the roof of the main station building, seen in the next picture. Two new giant high-rise buildings have been constructed either side of it, completely dwarfing it. The first is a Travelodge and the second, still being built when this shot was taken, looks like new apartments. When this station first opened in 1870, Walthamstow was a little village in Essex! (*Fuji X-S1*)

10 January 2020. The addition of a giant sundial outside the main station building at Walthamstow Central does nothing except highlight the fact that much of this station is now cast in shade from the high-rise buildings either side of it. Opened as Hoe Street in 1870, this building was originally built for the single line to the original terminus at Shern Hall Street, the next station down. The line was doubled shortly afterwards, in 1873, and the station was renamed Walthamstow Central in 1968, a few months before the London Underground Victoria Line opened for business the other side of the station. (*Canon 750d*)

20 April 2019. No. 315 807 comes to a stop at Wood Street Station. This station opened in 1873 as a replacement for the very short-lived Shern Hall Street terminus, which was situated a little further west. All the stations on this route have generous-length platforms, thanks to their Great Eastern Origins, so can comfortably fit the four and 8-car electric multiple units we see today, as opposed to the original long suburban trains hauled by the iconic Great Eastern N7 Steam locomotives. (*Fuji X-S1*)

20 April 2019. Rounding the curve into Wood Street Station from the direction of Liverpool Street is 4-car 317 710. The black triangle on the cab front is an interesting feature here because it denotes, in railway terms, that this is the end which would have had a first-class compartment. Though London Overground trains don't have first class on their train services, it was probably left over from the period when these units were inherited from Greater Anglia Railways. (*Fuji X-S1*)

20 April 2019. A nice study of Highams Park Station designed by Neville Ashbee. The station opened in 1873 as Hale End before becoming Highams Park and Hale End in 1894, with the second part of the name being finally dropped in 1969. This is actually the second station building on this spot, replacing the earlier version as far back as 1900. Initially the least used on the route, passenger usage has amazingly jumped by almost a million passengers from 2014 to 2019! (*Fuji X-S1*)

20 November 2019. The setting winter sun catches the top half of Highams Park Signal Box. Replacing an earlier one in 1925 that was further south, it was last used to just operate the barriers of the level crossing below. It was scheduled for demolition in 2002 when the barriers became remote controlled, but a campaign by local people ended up saving it. It then became the home to La Boîte Crêperie, although this seems to have closed (for the time being anyway) due to renovation work needing to be done. (*Canon 750d*)

20 April 2019. No. 315 804 with its modified headlight design runs into Highams Park Station from Chingford in bright sunshine. Highams Park owes its modern-day urbanisation and expansion in large part to the British Xylonite Company who became Halex. They were, in their day, one of the largest plastic manufacturers in the world. When they moved their factory here from Homerton they put Highams Park on the map, and in the past, if any reader played table tennis, the chances are the balls were made here! (*Fuji X-S1*)

20 April 2019. No. 315 815 approaches Chingford Station past the carriage washing plant and some of the carriage sidings situated here at the end of the line. More and larger carriage sidings are located next to the station platforms. This is where the majority of the class 315 and 317 stock that was used on the Lea Valley Lines is stabled overnight and between shifts. (*Fuji X-S1*)

20 April 2019. A scene that is now history, where two types of London Overground class 317 units, a 317/7 on the left, with a 317/8 on the right, sit stabled in the smaller of the two carriage yards at Chingford. The horns on the 317/7 series were moved below buffer beam height when they had their front ends modified. The carriage washing plant is on the left. (*Fuji X-S1*)

25 June 2020. Looking in the opposite direction to the previous picture, we see the new order on the Lea Valley Lines leaving Platform 1 at Chingford and crossing over onto the up line in the direction of London. When finishing this book, the author took one last trip over this route and found that the class 710s had only just begun to make their presence felt on it. Being a weekday, the carriage yards are empty, but the track layout is a modeller's dream! (*Canon 750d*)

20 April 2019. No. 315 814 has just conveyed the author to the end of the line here at Chingford. Some 317 stock can be seen stabled in the sidings alongside. The original Chingford Station, opened in 1873, was on the approach to the current station, beyond the carriage sidings in the previous picture. This new one, opened in 1878, was built closer to Epping Forest, with an extension to High Beech, deep in the forest, in mind. However, when Queen Victoria visited Chingford in 1882 she declared Epping Forest open to the public, thereby stifling any large future development through it! So this is where the line ends today. (*Fuji X-S1*)

25 June 2020. The old and the new on the stops at Chingford Station. No. 315 810 sits alongside two 4-car 710s working in multiple. There is approximately 37 years' age difference between them, the 315 being built by British Railway Engineering Ltd in York at the start of the 1980s, and the 710 being built by Bombardier Transportation at Derby around 2017. The station was undergoing something of a refurbishment when this photo was taken, hence the scaffolding. (Canon 750d)

Chapter Seven

North London Line

When Network Southeast (NSE) was set up as the London and South Eastern Passenger arm of British Rail in 1982, it inherited the North London rail routes mentioned in the introduction. These came under the generic title of the North London Lines. However, looking more specifically, we will start with the North London Line (NLL) proper; the route from Richmond to Stratford as we know it today in its current London Overground incarnation. Named and marketed in BR and NSE days as the 'Crosstown Link Line' and 'North London Link', it is in fact, as is the Overground itself, a collection of lines that over its early years have been merged and joined together. These have contracted, expanded and contracted again as passenger numbers, politics and finance have dictated. The very fact that the line itself, as far as fare-paying passengers are concerned, has survived and is now thriving, is remarkable in itself, considering it has fought off closure not once but twice. Firstly in the 1960s as part of the 'Beeching Axe' and secondly in the 70s by British Rail. The mobilisation of passenger and some political power along its route ultimately saved it. Under NSE ownership, things improved even more with the introduction of a 20-minute service and station improvements. With rail privatisation taking place in the mid-90s, the line was then transferred to Silverlink Metro.

However, recent history would mean starting with the closure of Broadstreet Station in 1986. The original terminus of the NLL sitting next door to Liverpool Street, it succumbed to the property developers and has now disappeared under the Bishopsgate office complex. But it was after this closure that the line from Dalston to North Woolwich via Stratford was electrified to enable end-to-end running from North Woolwich in east London all the way to Richmond in west London. It was always quite an interesting journey to take around the top of the capital along its 22-mile route and its 27 stations. But at the end of 2006, in preparation of the route being transferred from Silverlink Metro to London Overground, the stretch between Stratford and North Woolwich closed. Much of this part of the route was then used by the Docklands Light Railway (DLR) extension to Stratford International and paralleled in its last couple of miles or so by the DLR extension to King George V. The track bed of this last stretch has now been incorporated into the southern section of Crossrail (or the Elizabeth Line) to Abbey Wood. This now gives us the line that we see today from Richmond to Stratford. When London Overground took over, stations were refurbished, modernised and even rebuilt. Many platforms were re-lengthened (where previously they had been cut back) to cater for new 4-coach and then longer 5-coach class 378 Electric Multiple Units (EMUs). An off peak service of a train every 15 minutes is usually run.

In the 1970s, the electrification of the line changed from the 630V DC fourth rail to 630V

DC third rail, except for the section between Richmond and Gunnersbury, which shared with the London Underground District Line, retained its fourth rail. The class 501 EMUs (that also worked the fourth rail Watford DC lines with the London Underground Bakerloo Line) working the NLL were then modified to work on the third rail. The successor to these units were the common Southern Region Class 416 EMUs 2EPBs which were able to operate up to the 750V DC we see today. However, the class 416 units were never popular because their 2-coach length as opposed to the three coaches of the 501s caused overcrowding in the peak hours. A little relief for passengers was found when 3-car class 313 EMUs were brought in when NSE ran the NLL pre-Silverlink metro. These were proper dual voltage EMUs and were able to work off the 25kv AC overhead wires and the 750V DC third rail. Today the line uses both 25kv AC and 750V DC as its power supply, but before overhead AC electrification was extended for most of the route (for the benefit of freight), drivers of the dual voltage units had to 'Pan Up' and 'Pan Down' at a number of locations to switch between the two. Now, drivers of the Overground class 378 EMUs introduced in 2010, just have to remember to 'Pan Up' or 'Pan Down' at Acton Central when leaving or entering third rail territory.

19 February 2016. No. 378 255, proudly boasting its 5-car train vinyl sits at Stratford's Platform 2, waiting to leave for its journey down the North London Line. Overground services at Stratford terminate at Platforms 1 and 2 which, though they are of roughly equal length, are staggered because of their design. Both are capable of taking trains longer than the current 5-car lengths. When the station was rebuilt for the new Westfield shopping centre and the 2012 Olympics, the original North London Line Platforms 1 & 2, on a lower level, were transferred to the Docklands Light Railway in around 2009, and became Platforms 16 & 17 instead. Though the footbridge in the picture crosses the station, it's purely for the use of shoppers and pedestrians. (*Fuji X-S1*)

17 March 2016. An unidentified class 378 rounds Channelsea Curve on its approach to Stratford Station. The Olympics may have taken place four years prior to this, but the development of the former goods depots, yards and works that Stratford was known for, continues apace, with all trace of the former now having been obliterated. Nowhere is this illustrated better than in Joe Brown's remarkable *London Railway Atlas 3rd edition*, where a comparison is made between the Stratford Station of 1951 and that of 2012. The lines to the left of the unit are used for freight on the North London Line, with a link far left to the Great Eastern Mainline via Carpenters Road Curve. (*Fuji X-S1*)

7 June 2020. Just before Hackney Wick is reached, the line crosses the River Lee Navigation. This is a section of the River Lea that has become converted into a canal. Apparently, the change in spelling can be attributed to this conversion! Bridges are plenty around this section, enabling some nice views on good days. Here, an unidentified class 378 has just left Hackney Wick in the direction of Stratford, which is a stone's throw away. The footpath under the bridge on the right is part of the 'Capital Ring', a circular walking route around London, organised into 15 sections between Woolwich and Becton District Park. (*Canon 750d*)

13 June 2020. Hackney Wick Station is relatively new in London railway terms, having opened in 1980. It replaced an earlier station further down the line called Victoria Park and Hackney Wick, which closed due to bomb damage in 1943. It was then completely rebuilt and modernised in 2017/2018 to the design that we see in the picture here. A new under-station walkway is due to open in 2020, improving access to the parts of Hackney Wick on the other side of the station. At present, something of a circular detour has to be made. (*Canon 750d*)

30 May 2019. Hackney Wick has a reputation for street art, murals and graffiti, so much so, in fact, that you can go on street art tours, taking in the various decorated buildings, streets and walls of the area. This mural, somewhat small in comparison to some of the other art in the area, depicts an artist's impression of the London Overground, and can be found on the Stratford bound platform at Hackney Wick Station. (*Fuji X-S1*)

30 May 2019. No. 378 202 rounds the curve into Hackney Wick. No. 202 is a 378/2 unit that was the second one built as part of a batch of dual voltage units to operate either on the DC third rail, or on the AC overhead electric power supply as we see here. Dual voltage 378s have been used on all the Overground routes except for the Lea Valley Lines, although they are mainly used on the North London Line and Watford DC lines. (*Fuji X-S1*)

30 May 2019. No. 378 230 takes the slight 'S' curve (the compression effect of the zoom makes it look sharper than it is) into Hackney Central Station over the A107/Mare Street road bridge, after having left Homerton Station. The service pattern on this section is very frequent, as six trains per hour go to Stratford, either from Clapham Junction or Richmond, with four trains per hour to Clapham Junction and two trains per hour to Richmond. A sizable amount of freight also runs along this stretch. (*Fuji X-S1*)

25 June 2020. No look at Hackney Central Station would be complete without a picture of the covered walkway at the end of Platform 2. This opened in July 2015 and connects Hackney Central with Hackney Downs Station on London Overground's Lea Valley Lines, above and to the right behind the trees. This link meant passengers no longer had to make a long circuitous detour between the two stations at street level. Certainly one of the more useful bits of infrastructure on this route! (*Canon 750d*)

30 May 2019. No. 378 257 approaches Hackney Central as another 378 disappears around the corner in the distance, heading for Dalston Kingsland. The point work between the two is Navarino Road Junction, while the track leading off to the left is the Graham Road Curve. This is a link that was built in 1986 so North London Line trains would have access to Liverpool Street Station when Broad Street closed, via the Lea Valley lines that run directly above. Graham Road Goods Depot was also situated here before it closed in 1965. (*Fuji X-S1*)

19 June 2020. Almost a meeting of 378s at Dalston Kingsland Station, as one 378 gets the green light to leave while another, approaching from Canonbury, takes the Dalston Western curve for Dalston Junction on the East London Line. The original station here opened in 1850, but closed in 1865 when Dalston Junction opened close by. This current station opened in 1983, three years before the original Dalston Junction closed (it reopened again in 2010). (*Canon 750d*)

6 July 2013. Freightliner 66 502 *Basford Hall Centenary 2001* powers through the cutting between Newington Green Road Bridge and Canonbury Road Bridge towards Canonbury Station. This sort of Freightliner traffic is the bread and butter of the North London line, bringing container traffic from the ports in the East of England, such as Felixstowe, across London and up the West Coast Mainline. (*Fuji X-S1*)

6 July 2019. No. 378 202 arrives at Canonbury Station on the North London Line side. The North London Line passenger services have used four main types of Electric Multiple Units over their more recent history, going back to the days of British Rail. Beginning with the class 501, then continuing with the class 416s, never hugely popular because of their 2-coach lengths. These then gave way to the class 313 under Network Southeast into Silverlink Metro before the London Overground 378s were introduced. (Fuji X-S1)

6 July 2019. Passengers throng the Stratford-bound Platform 8 at Highbury and Islington, waiting for the next service, while the author stands on Platform 7. The station was built with four surface platforms, but suffered heavily during the war and post-war, contracting to just Platforms 1 & 2. These are out of shot to the right, with an 'emergency platform' where the author is standing. Freight trains used this line until they started using the passenger lines in the 80s. When the East London Line was extended here in 2011, terminating in Platforms 1 & 2, the North London Line (and freight) went back to using newly-rebuilt Platforms 7 & 8. So what of Platforms 3 to 6? They serve the Victoria Line and Great Northern Line below ground! (Fuji X-S1)

17 April 2019. No. 378 210 comes into Platform 2 at Caledonian Road and Barnsbury Station. In common with many stations on the North London Line, the current one bears little resemblance to what lay before. Four platforms have now become an island (curiously numbered 2 & 3 with no Platform 1), and all traces of any platform buildings have long been swept away. What the Luftwaffe failed to do in the Second World War, British Rail completed in the '60s. The footbridge in the picture, complete with accessible lifts, is the only thing of any note at this station; and even this is reached from a *very* long footpath from the Caledonian Road. Progress, eh? (*Canon 750d*)

23 January 2020. On an overcast morning, the Network Rail Windhoff Overhead Line Equipment train, DR 98003, approaches Caledonian Road and Barnsbury from the direction of Willesden Junction, on the outside freight line. This was just hours after a catastrophic derailment of a freight train on the Gospel Oak to Barking Line had done enormous damage and shut the line. Perhaps 98003 is going to or has come from the scene? In any case it's safe to assume it's going to be needed there at some point! (*Canon 750d*)

10 January 2020. Camden Road Station from Bonny Street. The circular red plaque next to the entrance is a 'Transport Trust Transport Heritage Site' plaque and reads as follows: 'CAMDEN ROAD STATION (formerly Camden Town). Opened 1870, one of six Italianate stations designed by Edwin Henry Horne for the fast-growing North London Railway.' Unlike the other similar Italianate stations on this line, this building has survived and is in good condition. (*Canon 750d*)

10 January 2020. *Professor Sir Peter Hall*, 378 204, arrives at Platform 2 at Camden Road in some afternoon winter sunshine, having just traversed Camden Road West Junction. Platform 2 used to be an island platform, with two more tracks and another platform behind the fence on the left of the picture. These were known as the No.1 lines and were often used by freight trains. They ran as far east as the short-lived York Way freightliner terminal, where the North London Line now grows from two to four tracks. They were taken out of service in the mid-80s, but might yet revert to public use and a green open space as the 'Camden Highline'. (*Canon 750d*)

21 February 2020. Veteran Freightliner AC electric locomotive 86 613 double heads a Freightliner working with a stablemate through Camden Road. Such double heading by class 86s on Freightliners is normal and they spend most of their time working in pairs. Just beyond the station, they will take the left fork and travel onto the West Coast Mainline via Primrose Hill. It's incredible to think that when these machines were first entering service on crack express West Coast passenger workings over 50 years ago, steam was still going! (*Canon 750d*)

17 April 2019. No. 378 205 enters Kentish Town West Station as a female passenger checks her phone. Kentish Town West opened in 1867, but didn't receive its 'West' suffix until 1924. The station was primarily made of wood and was so severely damaged by fire in April 1971 that it was closed. It wasn't until 1976 that the decision was taken to make this closure permanent. However, a hard-fought campaign was launched to reopen it and did so in 1981. Its basic and spartan look never really changed between the old and new stations. (*Canon 750d*)

1 February 2019. A couple of track workers wait for 378 234 to cross Gospel Oak Junction on the North London line, about to pull into Platform 2 at Gospel Oak on a cold winters day after a light dusting of snow. The junction was installed here, linking the Gospel Oak line to the North London Line in 1916 for wartime use, before being removed in 1922. It was re-laid again for the Second World War and then became a permanent fixture. These days it's heavily used by freight and empty coaching stock, traversing one from one line to the other. (*Canon 750d*)

15 April 2019. A member of staff confers with the driver of 378 218 as it stands at Platform 1 at Gospel Oak Station. A useful addition here would be a footbridge between the slightly staggered Platforms 1 and 2, as at the current time the public have to use a deep level subway reached by two long flights of steps. Or, failing that, they could take the lift that is situated at the end of the platforms in the distance. (*Fuji X-S1*)

7 February 2020. The fruit and veg seller outside Hampstead Heath Station is doing a brisk trade on a chilly afternoon as a sign inside the station entrance warns passengers of the ongoing disruption caused by the freight train derailment on the Gospel Oak to Barking Line. This station is popular with people visiting the heath, and the short walk to Parliament Hill up the road to the left of the station affords good views over the city of London. The poet John Keats also lived around the corner and his former home is now a museum. (*Canon 750d*)

21 February 2020. No. 378 210 emerges from Hampstead Tunnel. At 1,166 yards long, the tunnel runs under Hampstead Hill, one of the highest points in London, and was opened in 1860. In 1985, a section of the retaining wall at the tunnel end of the down platform collapsed during a landslip that temporarily blocked the line. During an 11-month closure of the line in 1996, major upgrade work was carried out, which included lowering the trackbed for extra clearance for the overhead catenary, and extra bracing, as seen here, to reinforce the walls. (*Canon 750d*)

15 April 2019. No. 378 201 bursts out of Hampstead Heath tunnel into sunshine at Finchley Road and Frognal Station at the other end from the previous shot. At one time, no fewer than three different Finchley Road Stations lined this side of Finchley Road, crossing above the train in this shot. The others were 'Finchley Road (for the Midland Railway)' and the Finchley Road Underground station serving the Jubilee and Metropolitan Lines. They were all within feet of each other, but the Midland Railway station closed in 1927 and the site has, in recent years, been buried under a cinema and supermarket complex. (*Fuji X-S1*)

16 April 2019. Having earlier left Willesden Junction, brand new 710 269 approaches Finchley Road and Frognal for a driver training and test run on the Gospel Oak to Barking Line. But first, in order to reach that line, these new units had to traverse this section of the North London Line from their depot at Willesden Junction. In the background can be seen the bridge that carries the North London Line over the Midland Mainline out of London St Pancras. (*Canon 750d*)

7 June 2020. Like Finchley Road in the past, the main road through West Hampstead has three stations all within yards of each other: West Hampstead Thameslink, this Overground station (called West End Lane until 1975) and the Underground station serving the Jubilee Line. Despite being modernised in 2007 when London Overground took over, the old station was in danger of becoming too small for the amount of traffic passing through it. So from 2015 to 2020, the station was completely rebuilt in stages to minimize impact on passengers. The new station entrance can be seen to the left of the old station building in the photo. This building was going to be demolished but, as it still retains the ticket office, and after public pressure, it's still standing! (*Canon 750d*)

23 January 2020. An unidentified class 378 in the new Overground livery (somewhat unusual on the North London Line at this time) pulls into West Hampstead Station. The two new widened staircases can be seen on either side of the photo, with new lifts behind them making the new station accessible. Also evident are the new platforms which are twice as wide as previously, with the drainage ducting down the middle of them – a good indicator as to how narrow the old ones used to be. This station alone sees more than four and a half million passengers a year, but plans and schemes to link all three stations in West Hampstead together to make one big interchange have never came to fruition. (*Canon 750d*)

15 April 2019. A brand new 710 263 approaches Brondesbury Station in some wonderful sunshine on the North London Line, after some driver training and testing on the Gospel Oak to Barking Line. The bridge in the background carries the Chiltern Line and the Metropolitan and Jubilee London Underground lines over the North London Line. (*Fuji X-S1*)

17 April 2019 No. 378 201 is about to run under the Brondesbury Park road bridge and then pull into Brondesbury Park Station. Though Brondesbury Station opened with the Hampstead Junction railway in 1860, it wasn't until a full 48 years later, in 1908, that Brondesbury Park was opened. Set in almost tranquil urban surroundings, a miniature golf course can be found nearby. (*Canon 750d*)

17 April 2019. Europhoenix/Rail Operations Group 37 611 *Pegasus* on stalking horse duties, following behind a new class 710 on driver training and testing on the Gospel Oak Line. 37 611 is no less than the fourth number this locomotive has had, as it started life as D6871 before becoming 37 171, then changing to 37 690 before finally becoming 37 611 *Pegasus*. Owned by the locomotive spot hire and refurbishing firm Europhoenix, it's among a number of class 37s leased to the Rail Operations Group. It's fitted with a Dellner coupler on it's front to enable it to move railway stock fitted likewise. (*Canon 750d*)

15 April 2019. No. 378 256 stands at Kensal Rise. The station originally opened in 1873 under the name of Kensal Green, further west. It was then moved east after 1873 and was renamed Kensal Rise in 1890. A large-sized gentleman's toilet block was situated in the 1960s just where the people are sitting on the platform bench, but this disappeared along with the platform canopies. The main platform buildings were situated on the downside, where the train is standing, and along with a signal box, these have all been swept away. (*Fuji X-S1*)

6 December 2019. An atmospheric shot after a winter storm, looking down Platform 5 of Willesden Junction High Level station towards Richmond and Clapham Junction. Not that you would realise it today, but a second line and platform were once located on the left for services to Earls Court. The platform and its buildings were demolished in the mid 50s, with the track being used for freight before disappearing shortly after. Leaving Willesden Junction, the North London Line bears to the right to continue onto Richmond. (*Fuji X-S1*)

26 June 2020. Upon leaving Willesden Junction, the North London Line diverges from the lines to Clapham Junction and crosses the Kew Curve Grand Canal Bridge over the Paddington section of the Grand Union Canal. Here, a class 378 is about to cross the bridge heading for Richmond. Just under the bridge can be seen the wharf owned by the Powerday recycling centre so they can transport waste by water! (*Canon 750d*)

8 December 2019. At Acton Central, drivers of the London Overground 378 units are reminded to 'Pan Up' on the up platform. A similar sign reminding them to 'Pan Down' can be seen at the end of the down platform. As this station is on the stretch where the third/fourth rail DC electrification joins the overhead 25kv AC overhead power supply, drivers must raise or lower the train's pantograph, depending if they are coming or going from one to the other. No. 378 228 runs into the down platform, the canopy of which was half destroyed by fire in 1981. (*Canon 750d*)

8 December 2019. No. 378 256 on the left and 378 204 on the right, heading towards Richmond, cross at South Acton Station. Once an interchange station, there is now no trace on the left, where the modern flats are, of the terminating point on an embankment of the South Acton Shuttle from Acton Town, or of the platform for the Hammersmith and Chiswick branch on the right. The former closed to passengers in 1959 and the latter in 1917, though freight continued to use it until 1965. (*Canon 750d*)

8 December 2019. Bollo Lane Junction Signal Box is a true survivor on the London railway network. So much so that it's now Grade II listed, though you might think otherwise, looking at it. Keen-eyed observers will notice that it still retains its Network SouthEast markings beneath the graffiti. Opened in 1878 by the London & South Western Railway, it's believed to be the only example of an LSWR Type II signal box still in existence. It is now dwarfed by the surrounding new-build blocks of offices and apartments that are slowly burying this past of South Acton. (*Canon 750d*)

17 February 2019. A nice overall view of Gunnersbury Station seen from the Wellesley Road bridge, as a class 378 arrives from Richmond. This station is shared with the London Underground District Line from the same destination. Originally a two-island and one-side platform station serving five tracks in a wide grass-lined cutting, it changed to a single island in the early 1930s. Not much changed from then until the mid-60s. This station was then lined by the two multi-story car parks in the photo, built on the old platforms. The office block built along with the development is the home of Clece Care Services and the British Standards Institute. (*Canon 750d*)

8 December 2019. An unidentified class 378 crosses Kew Bridge (otherwise known as Strand on the Green Bridge) across the River Thames on a cold and dull winter's day. Made out of wrought iron, at 575 feet long it was designed by W. R. Galbraith for the London and South Western Railway. It was opened in 1869 and is now Grade II listed. Of interest are a Second World War pillbox situated at the south end that can be seen from a train, and a house on the Thames river side where this photo was taken, that was once the home of actor Donald Pleasence. (*Canon 750d*)

8 December 2019. Kew Gardens Station is not only the stop for the world-famous botanical gardens, but it has a Grade II listed station building (seen through the legs of the bridge) and footbridge as well. The footbridge was opened in 1912 and was one of the earliest forms of reinforced concrete used in the country at the time, with a method pioneered by the French engineer, Francois Hennebique. Its high sides were built to protect people using the bridge from the soot and steam of passing steam trains. Today, a subway is also available. (*Canon 750d*)

8 December 2019. No. 378 256 leaves Kew Gardens Station in bright sunshine with the footbridge from the previous picture seen to another advantage. The platforms here are a lot longer than the five cars of the London Overground 378 units, as they are also used by London Underground District Line S7 trains, which are seven cars long. (*Canon 750d*)

18 June 2016. No. 378 208, boasting its 5-car capacity, approaches Richmond Station and lines up neatly with a London Underground District Line train of S7 Stock that has just departed. The signal box is Richmond Signal Box, which is still in use. The lines on the far right are the South Western Railway through lines from/to London Waterloo Station. The view from this bridge outside the station has changed greatly since the 1970s/80s. Gone are the bus depot and the large blue gas holder to be replaced with low rise flats as seen here, and rows of suburban houses. (*Fuji X-S1*)

27 January 2020. The lights are on in Richmond Signal Box, at just gone 8pm in the evening. A London Overground class 378 passes by and lines up for Platform 4 at Richmond Station. In the distance, a South Western Railways train has not long left North Sheen Station, just seen beyond the footbridge at the top of the picture. The very tip of 'The Shard', one of the tallest buildings in Europe, at London Bridge, can also be glimpsed above the signal box. (*Canon 750d*)

27 January 2020. No. 378 231 sits at Platform 4 in Richmond Station, its journey now at an end. London Overground services use Platforms 3, 4 and 5 at Richmond, London Underground District Line services use Platforms 6 and 7, while South Western Railway services use the through Platforms 1 and 2 on the far right of the picture. The scourge of the ever-present chewing gum can be seen here as well! (*Canon 750d*)

Chapter Eight

Romford to Upminster

The last London Overground route is unquestionably the shortest and most unique on the network. At approx. 3.4 miles in length, the Romford to Upminster line only has one intermediate station at Emerson Park. Running within a single fare zone, Zone 6, it's single track throughout and takes a mere nine minutes to travel from one end to the other, with two trains per hour. Looking at it on a map, you would think that it's completely estranged from the rest of the Overground network, such is its isolation. Known locally as the 'Romford Push and Pull', it opened in 1893 as a branch of the former London, Tilbury and Southend Railway (LTS), now c2c and London Underground District Line, at Upminster.

It linked with the Great Eastern mainline at Romford for its freight yard there. A large housing estate built at Emerson Park at the end of the 1800s was another reason for the line being built. However, the LTS was so concerned about the inhabitants travelling to Romford for onward travel to London that a loop was built not far from Emerson Park so trains could return to Upminster! When push-pull trains began working on the route, the loop went in 1936. Facing possible closure in the 60s, it wasn't until 1986 that the line was electrified at 25kv AC overhead, previously with Diesel Multiple Units working on it. It was then worked by class 315s under Abellio Greater Anglia before it was transferred to London Overground in 2015.

6 July 2019. We start our journey on the Romford to Upminster line, looking back at Platform 2 on Romford Station, that serves TfL Rail and Greater Anglia services out of London Liverpool Street. The Overground platform is Platform 1 but is a little separate from the rest of Romford Station, being in a bay platform at the country end of Platform 2. Access is via this walkway. (*Fuji X-S1*)

6 July 2019. Passengers wait to board 315 811 as it draws up to the buffer stops at Platform 1, Romford Station. It might have been an overcast day, but it was very hot and humid as their attire points out. Platform 1 was, for most of its years, a substantial wooden affair, but was finally made more substantial still, being replaced by a concrete one in 1989. The class 315s that ply this route back and forth all day are based at Ilford depot. (*Fuji X-S1*)

6 July 2019. No. 315 811 is about to pass under the road bridge that carries Butts Green Road into North Street at Emerson Park Station. Looking very much like a country branch line, it was only ever single track. However, a run round loop was situated just beyond the last carriage, so that trains from Upminster on the London, Tilbury and Southend line could return to Upminster. This was done in a bid to 'persuade' passengers not to use the rival Great Eastern railway company's station at Romford! The loop disappeared in 1936 after 'push pull' working began on the line. (*Fuji X-S1*)

6 July 2019. Emerson Park Station, looking like a country halt serving a country branch line. The station in large part came about because of a housing estate being built nearby at the start of the 1900s. It's a simple affair, having lost its platform booking office to fire in the '80s. And yet it's pleasing to see that such a small station is still staffed, and when the author visited, the 'station master' was only too keen to show his recently planted flowerbeds in the picture. Well cared for indeed! (*Fuji X-S1*)

6 July 2019. No. 315 811 approaches Upminster Station having almost, but not quite, joined the London Underground's District Line formation on the left. The C2C tracks are far left in the distance. The train has taken nine minutes to reach this point from Romford, the shortest line and distance on the London Overground network. The line, worked by Diesel Multiple Units after steam, faced an uncertain future in the mid-1980s, but was saved by its electrification. (*Fuji X-S1*)

6 July 2019. No. 315 811 sits at Platform 6 at Upminster Station, awaiting its return journey back to Romford. In time, these 315 EMUs would be replaced by new class 710 'Aventras' on the route, and at the time of writing, the platform stop boards for these new units are already in place. Passenger loadings on the line are never big and a four-coach train is more than ample for the traffic it sees. (*Fuji X-S1*)

Chapter Nine

South London Line

In its original form, the South London Line (SLL) ran for 8.5 miles from London Victoria station to London Bridge Station via Denmark Hill. Something of a semi-circle around the bottom southeastern corner of London, it linked two of London's biggest Southern Railway termini. It was also a pioneer in electric traction when, in a bid to win custom back from the local tramways, it switched to an overhead AC power supply in 1909. While it was successful, at 6700 volts, it was seen as non-standard, and in 1928 the route was converted to the third rail that we find on the Southern Region today. This route, previous to London Overground, was operated by Southern with 2-car class 456s on what was basically a half-hour shuttle service. It was especially useful to the south London communities along its route, especially for those that used Kings College Hospital at Denmark Hill. The South London Line under London Overground that we see today, however, is somewhat different. At the Victoria end, the route was diverted over existing track after leaving Wandsworth Road at Factory Junction. It then ran under the lines out of Victoria and Waterloo via Longhedge Junction and Pouparts Junction before running up to terminate at Clapham Junction, linking it to the West London Line. The other end of the route towards London Bridge entailed linking it with the newly refurbished East London line at Surrey Quays. Fortunately the trackbed of the old East London Railway could be used to bridge this gap from Old Kent Road Junction to Silwood Junction on the East London Line. It was because of these changes that it could now be argued, more so than the other routes absorbed into the London Overground, that the South London Line has now ceased to exist entirely. 'Unhooking' the line from its two original destinations at either end then diverting those ends to connect with the West London Line and East London Line instead proved to be not entirely popular. Looking at it on the map, the closing of the circle in the bottom half of the capital would make sense, enabling the Overground to become a truly orbital railway. But in so doing, it robbed this part of South London of an important commuter service, and a passenger and political campaign was waged to save it. Ultimately though, this campaign failed against the now unstoppable expansion of the Overground network. And as if to rub salt into the wound, the route is no longer referred to as the South London Line, but instead as part of the East London Line, officially as the 'East London Line Extension (Phase 2)' The last Southern SLL service ran in December 2012 when the new link was opened and London Overground began to run over the route.

4 February 2017 sees 378 206 traversing the stretch of line between Pouparts Junction and Longhedge Junction, having already came via Lavender Hill Junction out of Clapham Junction! Such is the myriad of lines and junctions out of Clapham, a good track atlas is a must for understanding them all. This unit is also emblazoned with the '5-Car Train' vinyl in the front of the cab, to advertise extra capacity on London Overground services, as four cars were slowly becoming five. On some units a whole coach was decked out with a vinyl being 'unwrapped' off of it. (*Fuji X-S1*)

3 April 2009. The way it used to be on the South London Line, before London Overground took over and changed both destinations of the route. Southern 2-car EMU 456 012 is about to arrive at Wandsworth Road, having come from London Victoria. In the background can be seen the blue MAN gasholder, now long since gone, and in the foreground, bottom right, can be seen the capped entrance to the old subway. (*Sony A100*)

14 June 2020. Battersea Park Station is not a station usually associated with the London Overground. But the station does serve it, at the time of writing, twice a day, in what can only be described as a *very* limited service of one very early morning and one very late night train. In 2016, the station even found its way onto the Overground Map, which caused a stir in London Railway circles. These are, of course, 'Parliamentary services' that London Overground is contractually obliged to run. The exception is when the Overground platforms at Clapham Junction are closed for engineering work, such as when this shot was taken early on a Sunday morning, when Overground services terminated here until 10.15am. No. 378 147 waits to leave for Highbury and Islington via Wandsworth Road. (*Canon 750d*)

21 January 2017. In a shot that would now be difficult because of the sheer amount of overgrowth that has grown up to become the bane of Britain's railways, 378 149 crosses the arches from Longhedge Junctions to Factory Junctions. The industrial buildings behind the train belong to London Concrete and Day Aggregates, who have a rail terminal here as well. (*Fuji X-S1*)

21 January 2017. No. 378 136 has just came off the Ludgate Lines top left from Clapham Junction and is coming over the spot where the Atlantic Lines join at Factory Junction, heading into Wandsworth Road Station. An 8-car Southeastern class 375 (with 622 on the rear) hurries past on its way to London Victoria. The large warehouse-type building in the top left corner is one of the sheds of Stewarts Lane depot. (*Fuji X-S1*)

21 January 2017 and 378 232, another recently lengthened 5-car unit, arrives at Wandsworth Road Station and some winter sunshine. Though the frost might have disappeared on the down platform, it still lingers in the shadows on the up. The first footbridge here at the other end of the station closed in 1928. A subway was then used before this closed in 1988, when the present footbridge was put in its place, redundant from Mitcham Station! (*Fuji X-S1*)

30 August 2019. An unidentified 378 in the new Overground livery, introduced in late 2018, arrives at Wandsworth Road Station. The skyline from the footbridge here has changed much over the recent years. Gone is the blue MAN gasholder, to be replaced by flats and apartments; and Battersea Power Station is undergoing its rebuilding and conversion into more flats and apartments for London's well-off. In the centre distance, a Southeastern 'Networker' hurries across the arches to London Victoria. (*Fuji X-S1*)

29 January 2020. No. 378 147, wearing the new Overground livery, arrives on Platform 1 at Wandsworth Road Station at around 6.30pm. Platform comfort is sparse at this station, with double the amount of shelters on Platform 1 than Platform 2. The lines passing on the left are the up and down Chatham Mainlines used by Southeastern services from Kent to London Victoria. (*Canon 750d*)

30 August 2019. GB Railfreight 66 780 *Cemex Express* roars through Clapham High Street just after midday on an aggregates train. Formerly a DB Cargo machine, it originally carried the number 66 008. At the time of writing, this is a one-off livery for Cemex, one of GBRfs customers that specialises in cement and ready-mix concrete. Although it was named after an aggregates company, it has been pictured working on all sorts of freight workings. (*Fuji X-S1*)

30 August 2019. The entrance to Clapham High Street Station. Rudimentary at best, although the bike shelter looks like a London Overground addition. The original large station buildings remain at platform level, but are no longer a part of the station itself, and are now used for other purposes, their canopies long since gone. Originally called Clapham Road, it had a change of name to the more accurate Clapham High Street in 1989. (*Fuji X-S1*)

30 August 2019. Re-liveried 378 147 pulls into Platform 1 at Denmark Hill Station in the early afternoon. The facilities at this station have been progressively modernised over the years and new lifts and walkways can be seen in the background. Being a large station of four platforms, one of its key attributes is that it's situated just a stone's throw from Kings College Hospital, over the road from the main building. (*Fuji X-S1*)

30 August 2019. The new footbridge and lifts at Denmark Hill enable a good overall view of the station as 378 208 pulls into Platform 2. The main station building seen above the platforms was built in Italianate style and was used as a mystical church in the 1920s. Up until the '70s, it fell into disrepair, and in 1980 a deliberate fire destroyed the roof. Facing demolition, it was restored and is now a Grade II listed public house. (*Fuji X-S1*)

30 August 2019. Almost a mirror image at Peckham Rye, as 378 141 shares the island Platform 1 & 2 with 378 230. Overground and Southern services use these platforms, while South Eastern and Thameslink services use Platforms 3 & 4, seen on the far left. This island platform replaced a smaller earlier one, abandoned in 1933. When it was rebuilt in 1961, it completely took over from two side platforms, which were then subsequently demolished. (*Fuji X-S1*)

30 August 2019. No. 378 208 arrives at Queens Road Peckham. Again, this is an island platform, built in 1977, that replaces an earlier smaller island platform and two side platforms. To the right of the train can be seen the towers and skyscrapers of Canary Wharf, in what was London's docklands. From here, the London Overground leaves the South London Line at Old Kent Road Junction and links up to the East London Line at Silwood Junction. (*Fuji X-S1*)

Chapter Ten

Watford DC Lines

The second of the North London Lines that were operated by Network South East and then by Silverlink Metro is the Watford DC Line. It was marketed by Network Southeast in 1988 as 'The Harlequin Line' when they wanted to give each of its routes a separate identity. 'Harlequin' was a mix of Harlesden and Queens Park stations when it was the winning entry in a competition. The 'DC' comes from the 'Direct Current' of its electricity supply. This is a legacy of its building by the London North Western Railway in 1912, using the 630V DC Fourth rail system which was (and still is) also used by the London Underground.

Built as a new line with extra capacity for suburban and outer suburban services in and out of Euston Station, it ran to Watford Junction and to a now closed branch to Croxley Green. It runs parallel with the AC overhead electrified West Coast Mainline that continues north. Some services also ran from Watford to Broadstreet and then to Liverpool Street when Broadstreet closed, via a connection to the North London Line at Primrose Hill. The Liverpool Street services were implemented via a new curve at Graham Road as a form of compensation for the loss of Broadstreet, but didn't last long, however. At Queens Park, the line is joined by the London Underground Bakerloo Line, and both Underground and Overground Trains share the tracks as far as Harrow and Wealdstone, where the Bakerloo Line terminates. Up until 1982, it had gone all the way to Watford Junction itself.

It was in the 1970s, alongside the rest of the North London Lines, that the line and the class 501 EMUs used on it were standardised to be electrified on the third rail system. The fourth rail was however left in place and working as far as Harrow and Wealdstone for the Bakerloo Line trains. Beyond this point, the fourth rail is still in existence, but now unmounted and disused. Every so often though, talk arises of re-extending the Bakerloo Line back to Watford Junction. Currently, the line has been electrified at 750V DC, which is standard across the Overground sections of the network that use the third rail. Leaving Bushey station, the line takes its only major detour on the grand curving Bushey viaduct over the River Colne. This is a throwback to when the line branched off to run to Croxley Green and Rickmansworth Church Street. The latter closed in 1952, but the former lasted until as late as 1995, when it saw just one trip a day on a dilapidated line to a station in such a state that a temporary platform was opened across the tracks! Curiously, the line was still 'legally' open until 2003, despite road improvement work having cut the embankment outside Croxley Green station, isolating it on an overgrown island next to the ring road! Track, however, was still *in situ* on this 'island' in 2013. Nearby Croxley depot serviced many of the Watford DC lines class 501s and Bakerloo Line tube stock until 1985, when the 501s were retired and the depot closed, future rolling stock being kept elsewhere. For years, however, London Underground's Metropolitan Line has wanted to extend the Watford end of their line to Watford Junction (currently, it falls somewhat short of the town centre at Cassiobury Park), using a lot of this route. Called the 'Croxley Rail Link', funding has always been an issue, though, and it remains a future project. After the class 501s came the class 313 EMUs introduced when NSE took over in 1986. Nearly identical class 508s, surplus from Merseyrail, could also be found on the line when Silverlink Metro took over. Both 313s and 508s ran until London Overground took the line over in 2007. Since then, class 378s have worked the route and latterly at the time of writing, brand new class 710s, software problems now resolved, have begun working the line and the majority of the services.

18 June 2009. The way it used to be at London Euston on the Watford DC Lines. No. 313 107 may be wearing the livery of Silverlink Metro, but upon closer inspection you will see a temporary London Overground name applied on the bodyside of the rearmost coach. The new class 378s had not yet been rolled out on this route and, in common with other parts of the new Overground network, Silverlink Metro's 313s were still being used, though marginally rebranded. (*Fuji 6500fd*)

23 April 2019. No. 378 213 sits at Platform 9 under the low-hanging roof of London Euston Station. In keeping with the electrification and modernisation of the West Coast Mainline in the late 50s, the demolition of the original Euston Station has gone down in railway history as a national disgrace. The station that we see today was opened in 1968 and is the fifth busiest station in the UK, serving Avanti West Coast, London North Western, London Overground and the Caledonian Sleeper. With the building of HS2, it's set to be changed still further. (*Fuji X-S1*)

23 April 2019 The interior of a Class 378/2 'Capitalstar' at London Euston Station. (The difference between 378/1s and 378/2s is that the former are third rail capable only, with the latter being dual voltage.) Although part of the very successful Bombardier 'Electrostar' family of Electric Multiple Units, they were specifically designed for the London Overground network. At first glance, the most noticeable difference from conventional train interiors is the tube style longitudinal seating that runs the length of the train. Introduced in 2009, they have progressively been lengthened from three to five cars as passenger numbers have grown. (*Fuji X-S1*)

23 April 2019. Having climbed Camden Bank and travelled through the 3,500 feet-long Primrose Hill Tunnel, 378 221 now exits into South Hampstead Station. The bridge over the fourth and fifth carriage carries the former Great Central, now Chiltern Railway, route out of London Marylebone. Originally called Loudoun Road, this station closed in 1917 to reopen in 1922 as South Hampstead. The more ornate portals of the tunnels for the adjacent West Coast Mainline can also just be made out. (*Fuji X-S1*)

23 April 2019. No. 378 257, as viewed though one of the arches of Loudoun Road bridge (hence the station's original name), carrying the entrance above for South Hampstead Station. The distinctive building seen in the background on the left is the rear of the Alexandra and Ainsworth Estate. Built in the 1970s, its brutalist architecture has been used in many TV programmes and films. (*Fuji X-S1*)

23 April 2019. No. 378 213 arrives at Kilburn High Road Station on an afternoon of cancellations on the Watford DC lines. Instead of the usual one train every 20 minutes, it had been over half an hour since the last Overground service had called here, bound for London Euston. Originally opened as Kilburn and Maida Vale in 1852, it originally had four platforms on all the main lines out of Euston. What we see today is all that's left, with the station now concentrated around the slow Watford DC lines; and the West Coast Mainline behind the fence on the left. (*Fuji X-S1*)

22 June 2020. No. 378 256, one of two 378s still running on the Watford DC lines at the time of writing, approaches Queens Park Station while passing the more southerly of the two London Underground Bakerloo Line sheds located here. Between them is the Bakerloo up and down lines. The Overground up line towards Euston is on the far left behind the shed. The West Coast Mainline is on the far right. (*Canon 750d*)

22 June 2020. Queens Park Station is an interesting station for the London Underground Bakerloo Line, but the London Overground lines flank it on either side. So here we turn our attention to 710 262, bound for Euston, running between the retaining wall and Platform 1. Interestingly, the platform edge flagstones are a long way from home, as they still bear the maker's name in places: 'Non Slip Stone Co, Halifax'! (*Canon 750d*)

23 April 2019. No. 378 257 emerges from the right hand bore of Kensal Green tunnel into Kensal Green Station. At 318 yards long, the tunnels take the line under Hazel Road open space, which fringes the vast expanse of Kensal Green Cemetery. Interestingly, many of the stations on the Watford DC lines serve both London Underground and London Overground services, but are run by the former, so the London Underground roundel takes precedent over the latter. (*Fuji X-S1*)

11 August 2018. No. 378 202 runs under the up and down North London Line platforms of Willesden Junction High Level into Platform 3 of Willesden Junction Low Level station. The line in the middle foreground runs into the bay Platform 2 which is used as a turn back and shunting line, so rarely sees passenger services. (*Fuji X-S1*)

22 June 2020. An unidentified class 710 comes to a stop at Harlesden Station in a shot taken from the once roofless and still windowless footbridge. The most noticeable thing about this station is that still retains its (almost) full length platform canopies. Opening in 1912, Harlesden Station is only a short walk from Willesden Junction. In the top left corner can be seen the floodlight towers that stand over Wembley freight yards and the Royal Mail terminal. (*Canon 750d*)

23 April 2019. No. 378 257 has just passed a northbound London Underground Bakerloo line train of 1972 stock while another one waits to come out from Stonebridge Park depot, which is located far in the background. Alstom Train care depot can also be seen to the left of the picture, while out of shot to the left and higher up are Wembley freight yards. (*Fuji X-S1*)

11 August 2018. North of Stonebridge Park and south of Wembley Central Station, the Watford DC Line/Bakerloo Line curves under the West Coast Mainline that 378 256 is about to take, heading for London Euston. This shot is taken from a long footbridge that crosses the Watford DC/Bakerloo Line, the West Coast Mainline and Wembley freight yards. (*Fuji X-S1*)

22 June 2020. Wembley Central Station has evolved a lot since its opening in 1837 and has been called in the past Sudbury, Sudbury and Wembley, Wembley for Sudbury before finally becoming Wembley Central in 1948. In the early 1950s, the station buildings were demolished and a huge concrete raft was laid over the station site so a shopping arcade could be built on top. This was then in turn demolished in 2008/2009 to make way for a new hotel and parade of shops. The current station entrance, adorned by all the services the station sees, and nondescript to say the least, takes up the far right corner of the parade beneath the hotel. (*Canon 750d*)

22 June 2020. The present-day London Underground and Overground platforms at Wembley Central. The concrete raft above can be seen entombing the station. All six of the lines here still have platforms, unlike many stations on this stretch of the West Coast Mainline out of Euston that have lost their platforms over time. However, Platforms 1 & 2 (in the picture) and 5 & 6 are the only ones used with any great frequency, especially for events at nearby Wembley Stadium. Platforms 3 & 4 are on the fast lines, so are rarely if ever used. (*Canon 750d*)

22 June 2020. No. 710 269 comes to a stop in North Wembley Station. Opened in 1912, it was going to be called East Lane, but North Wembley found more favour, and it was opened as such. It's almost identical to Kenton Station two stops along, and though station buildings are evident on both platforms, they are no longer used by the public. The ticket office is next to the footbridge above the rear coach of the train. (*Canon 750d*)

27 February 2020. South Kenton is an island platform, set alongside the West Coast Mainline; and here we see the new order on the Watford DC lines, with a Watford Junction-bound class 710 on the left with another, 710 263, bound for London Euston on the right. Class 710s began to take over the Watford DC lines from the Class 378s in late 2019 and, at the time of writing, had all but taken over the workings on this route save for one, possibly two, 378s still running. (*Canon 750d*)

22 June 2020. South Kenton Station is accessed from an underpass beneath the West Coast Mainline and London Underground/Overground lines that lead to the platforms above. No. 710 262 is leaving the station, heading for Watford Junction on a clear blue sky day that also sees the contrail of a plane passing overhead. A short walk across the playing fields here will take you to Northwick Park Station on the London Underground Metropolitan line. (*Canon 750d*)

1 March 2018. It may have been March, but winter still had a sting in its tale in 2018, with what was then known as the 'Beast from the East'. Snow has begun to fall, but the winds have not yet blown it over the West Coast Mainline; only the Watford DC/Bakerloo lines, as 378 213 passes Northwick Park, having left South Kenton in the background. Another 378 has just arrived there. (*Fuji X-S1*)

23 January 2015. Providing the backdrop of the second out of two places on the London Overground network passing beneath the London Underground, a Metropolitan Line S-Stock, either about to stop at Northwick Park, or having just left, passes over 378 227 approaching South Kenton. Chiltern Railway services also use the bridge in the background on services to and from Aylesbury via Harrow on the Hill. (*Fuji X-S1*)

13 March 2015. On the other side of the London Underground Metropolitan line lies another footbridge from where this picture was taken, looking down onto Kenton Station. With some degree of lucky timing, we see an Overground 378 (219) alongside a 1972 stock of the Bakerloo Line on the 'New Lines'. Simultaneously, a Virgin West Coast class 390 'Pendolino' duels with a London Midland class 350 'Desiro' on the Westcoast Mainline. Such is progress, the latter two railway companies no longer exist and are being replaced by Avanti West Coast and London Northwestern Railway. (*Fuji X-S1*)

9 February 2019. Moving on four years from the previous shot, we are now at Kenton Station and can see that the footbridge has been painted. The 1972 stock is now northbound, and the Overground 378 is now southbound towards London. But this shot gives another good indication of the size difference between the two. Kenton Station opened in 1912 and is typical of the stations on this stretch of the Watford DC 'New Lines'. (*Canon 750d*)

29 July 2016. No. 378 204 is nicely framed by some buddleia from another footbridge, this time outside Kenton Station. This type of flower is not only a nightmare for railway maintenance, but it so very often gets in the way of railway photography, such is its proliferation. Many railway enthusiasts will testify that it can and does grow everywhere around the railway. (*Fuji X-S1*)

4 August 2016. Looking in the opposite direction from the previous shot, we see 378 219 about to be passed by a Virgin Westcoast class 390 'Pendolino' on the West Coast Mainline up fast line. And like 378 204 in the previous shot, 219 is wearing its cab front vinyl of 'Overground 5 Car Train'. These stickers were progressively phased out when 5-car 378s became the norm across the Overground Network. (*Fuji X-S1*)

19 March 2015. No.378 255, a 4-car, arrives at a busy Platform 1, Harrow and Wealdstone Station, on a cold morning. All running lines here, like Wembley Central, have platforms, but also like Wembley Central, the West Coast Mainline fast lines are rarely used and have actually been fenced off to deter people contemplating suicide. Other than the London Underground/ Overground platforms, pictured, only 5 & 6 see regular stopping services. (*Fuji X-S1*)

24 June 2020. The up side station building at Harrow and Wealdstone Station, opened in 1911. To anyone with a knowledge of Britain's railways, Harrow and Wealdstone will always sadly be remembered as the scene of England's worst ever railway disaster, which claimed 112 lives. On 8 October 1952, an express train ran through danger signals into the back of a local train at Platform 4. Seconds later, a third train collided with the wreckage. The rather small memorial plaque to this event can be seen on the corner of the building beneath the TfL and BR symbols. (*Canon 750d*)

24 June 2020. The footbridge at Harrow and Wealdstone has recently been refurbished and is now completely accessible. It also gives good views of the Watford DC lines and West Coast Mainline heading north. The author was lucky to get this shot here, with no less than five trains on the lines, the only stationary one being the London Underground Bakerloo Line 1972 stock, second from left, waiting to return to service in the turn back. The others are an Overground 378 heading north, an Overground 710 heading south and, in the background, a Southern 377 has just departed, while the back of a freightliner can be seen, heading through the station. (*Canon 750d*)

27 August 2019. Hatch End station is two stops on from Harrow and Wealdstone station after Headstone Lane station. The original station here opened in about 1843 and was first called Pinner, later becoming Pinner and Hatch End in 1897. It then had a reversal to Hatch End for Pinner in 1920 before finally becoming Hatch End in 1956. The present station has a main station building dating from 1911 and is a very good example of London and North Western Railway architecture by Gerald Horsley. This affair is in stark contrast to the more modern station building on the up side. (*Canon 750d*)

27 February 2020. No. 710 265 is about to come to a stop at Hatch End Station. Hatch End can be seen as an end of this line in a couple of respects, as it's the end of the line in Middlesex and is seen as the end of the line in the London area. Beyond this station going north, Overground passengers travel to one of only three places on the London travel zone map outside Zone 6. Also to be noted is that the rear of the main station building here has kept its canopy whereas the front, seen in the previous photo, has lost the small one it had. (*Canon 750d*)

24 June 2020. When Carpenders Park opened in 1914, it was situated in open fields accessed via a footpath. Its two wooden platforms and footbridge were demolished in 1952 when a new island platform station, slightly further south, was opened, now reached via a tunnel under all the lines from a public square. This is the tunnel we see in the picture, while an Avanti West Coast 'Pendolino' races by on the fast line over the top. (*Canon 750d*)

24 June 2020. Once inside the tunnel, passengers are faced with this inclined ramp up to the ticket office and platforms in the distance. The orange handrails here give an indication to the railway company that now serves this station. London Underground Bakerloo Line services ceased calling here in 1982, when the Underground service to Watford Junction was cut back. (*Canon 750d*)

27 February 2020. One good aspect of the station at Carpenders Park now being an island platform is that it now affords good views 'under the wires' of passing passenger and freight trains on the West Coast Mainline. Here we see Freightliner 66 604 catching the afternoon sun about to pass the station with a trainload of matching hoppers. It's easy to see why class 66s are called 'Sheds'! (*Canon 750d*)

6 October 2019. An unidentified 378 leaves the sun behind it for a moment as it heads towards Carpenders Park, with Bushey Station being in the background beyond the bridge. This bridge carries the Watford Heath road across the tracks where it joins Oxhey Road just after the last arch on the left. As can be seen in the picture, this last arch was something of an afterthought when the New Lines/Watford DC lines were laid through here in 1911, so doesn't fit in with the rest of the bridge. (*Fuji X-S1*)

24 June 2020. Bushey Station is quite a curious one as the Overground/Watford DC line Platforms 1 & 2 curve away from the main station at the eastern end of the Bushey Viaduct. The mainline platforms behind them serve the fast and slow lines of the West Coast Mainline, though, as is modern practice, the fast line platforms are rarely used. Both up and down side station buildings are still both used. Though both very similar, the upside one, pictured, is the larger of the two and is sporting a clock tower. The down side one and the Overground platforms are reached via a subway inside. (*Canon 750d*)

28 September 2019. The class 710 'Aventras' had been running on the Watford DC lines a little under 20 days, when this shot was taken of 710 263 stopping at the sharply curving Overground platforms of Bushey Station. This is where the Watford DC lines leave their parallel course with the West Coast Mainline on a deviation over the arches of the Bushey Viaduct. (*Fuji X-S1*)

27 October 2019. There are two arched viaducts over the River Colne in Watford. One of five arches on the West Coast Mainline to the north east of the town, and this one, built on a curve of 13 arches which carries the London Overground to Watford Junction. This is something of a deviation on this stretch of the line as, after exiting the bridge, a triangle was formed, joining up with the Croxley Green Branch and Rickmansworth Branch, now both closed, though the former only as recently as the early '90s. Continuing on, the line makes another curve back on itself into Watford High Street Station before curving away once again to meet back up with the main line into Watford Junction. (*Canon 750d*)

22 September 2019. No. 378 229 is heading onto the Bushey Curve past the former Watford High Street Junction, with the now closed Croxley Green and Rickmansworth Branches forming two sides of a former triangle here. The bottom of the triangle was the Croxley Green Curve. The track bed of the Rickmansworth Branch exists as a walk and cycle path, but the route of the Croxley Green Branch is in limbo, awaiting funding to incorporate it into a London Underground Metropolitan Line extension to Watford Junction. Someday this curve might be a junction again… (*Fuji X-S1*)

24 June 2020. Watford is a big enough conurbation to have three stations. It used to have five if you include Watford Stadium and Watford West on the now defunct Croxley Green Branch. But currently, it has Watford Junction, Watford London Underground (for the Metropolitan Line) and this station, Watford High Street, serving the London Overground. A nice station where the main canopy is mostly supported on the braces between the retaining walls. Originally a single platform when opened in 1862, it changed to an island platform layout when the line was later doubled. (*Canon 750d*)

28 September 2019. Nos. 378 214 and 378 212 eye up a new class 710 at the Overground Platforms at an overcast Watford Junction, the end of the Watford DC Lines. Watford Junction has no less than 10 platforms serving London Overground, Avanti West Coast, London Northwestern Railway, Southern and even the Caledonian Sleeper. In the past, it was also the terminus for the London Underground Bakerloo Line, Croxley Green Branch and the Rickmansworth Branch. (*Fuji X-S1*)

Chapter Eleven

West London Line

The West London Line, from Clapham Junction to Willesden Junction, was the fourth in the collection of lines under the 'North London Lines' banner. Taken over by Silverlink Metro in 1997, in its current form it's the youngest, with two out of the six stations on its route, Shepherds Bush and Imperial Wharf, being opened in 2008 and 2009 respectively. The route itself, being the original West London Extension Railway, can be traced back to the mid nineteenth century, and was closed as a regular passenger line in 1940. This was found necessary owing to a culmination of bomb damage to many of its stations and a downturn in passengers, due to the nearby London Underground District Line and local trams. It was still heavily used by freight, especially coming from the south across the Thames at Battersea/Chelsea Harbour, and by long distance cross-London passenger services. A special shuttle service from Clapham Junction for the Post Office workers at Olympia used it as well. Nicknamed the 'Kenny Belle', this was unadvertised, and in modern day parlance would be called a 'Ghost Train'. It was also the last steam passenger service in London!

But it wasn't until the late 80s that a limited Clapham Junction–Kensington Olympia public service that *was* advertised began to be run. When in 1994 Network Southeast took control, revitalising London Railway services, it began to run a passenger service along its entire length, again using Diesel Multiple Units. In 1993, the line was electrified at 750V DC on the third rail, to enable Eurostar trains to and from Waterloo to use it to gain access to the Eurostar North Pole depot outside Willesden Junction. Beyond this point, passenger services 'Pan Up' on the approach to the high level station at Willesden Junction to use the 25kv AC overhead power supply where the West joins the North London Line. In 1997, Silverlink Metro took control and ran class 313 EMUs on the route. A new station at West Brompton was reopened on the site of the long since demolished old station, closed in 1940, adjacent to the District Line station. In 2007, the route was taken over by London Overground, who instigated a major improvement of the route to bring it in line with the rest of the Overground network. New stations at Imperial Wharf and Shepherds Bush opened soon after, both in large part funded by the landowners developing new apartments at the former and the Westfield shopping centre at the latter. At Clapham Junction, London Overground services often ran into Platform 17 having run under the junction. When the London Overground got their own dedicated platforms on Platform 2 and a rebuilt Platform 1 in later years, west London services terminate on the new Platform 1 a little ahead and to the side of the South London Line services on Platform 2.

9 January 2010. No. 378 015 has just left Clapham Junction and is about to cross onto Ludgate Junction to descend onto the West London Line after a light snow fall, not long after New Year 2010. The London Overground was only three years old by the time this shot was taken, which explains the short 3-carriage formation. In the old days, the first stop would have been the West London Battersea Station, but this closed for good in 1940, so the next modern day stop is Imperial Wharf across the River Thames. (*Sony A100*)

9 June 2020. Not long after having left Clapham Junction, the West London Line crosses the River Thames on Battersea Railway Bridge. Formally known as the Cremorne Bridge after the nearby riverside gardens in Chelsea, it's also known as Battersea New Bridge and by Network Rail (who own it) as the Chelsea River Bridge. Designed by William Baker, the chief engineer of the London and North Western Railway, it was opened in March 1863. Its five 120 foot lattice girder arches are set on stone piers and it is Grade II listed. (*Canon 750d*)

9 June 2020. Imperial Wharf Station is an entirely new station built for the London Overground and opened in 2009. It's situated on the approach arches to Battersea Rail Bridge high on an embankment, and was paid for by the two main companies engaged in building the Imperial Wharf housing and apartment complex around the station. So close is it however to Chelsea Harbour that this name was at first mooted as being the name for the station. It fulfils quite a need for a station here, as the previous station is across the Thames at Clapham and the next station on the line is West Brompton. Not a short walk away! (*Canon 750d*)

27 November 2019. No. 378 212 sits at Imperial Wharf Station on a bitterly cold November night, bound for Stratford and having not long left Clapham Junction. Aside from cross London freight, Southern serves these platforms as well with northbound services to Shepherds Bush, Watford Junction and Milton Keynes Central; and a southbound service to South Croydon. (*Fuji X-S1*)

22 January 2020. No. 378 218 comes to a stand at West Brompton on a wet drizzly afternoon. Like the other stations on the West London Line, West Brompton was closed in 1940 due to bomb damage, with the remains hanging on until the late '50s. By the '70s, the site had all but been cleared. It wasn't until January 1999 that a new station, seen here, was finally opened by the then Minister for Transport, Glenda Jackson. The London Underground District Line station runs alongside out of shot on the left. (*Canon 750d*)

9 June 2020. No. 378 2— has just left West Brompton in the distance and is heading for Kensington Olympia. It has just crossed over London Underground's West Kensington East Junction beneath it where the District Line divides for Hammersmith and Kensington Olympia. The tracks for Kensington Olympia are the ones that continue straight on towards the photographer, parallel with the Overground Lines but at a lower level. These days only a limited service is run over them. Lillie Bridge London Underground Depot for the District Line can also be seen on the right and behind that is the iconic tower block, the Empress State Building, which is currently the home of the Metropolitan Police. (*Canon 750d*)

19 February 2015. Nos. 378 216 and 378 220 sit at Kensington Olympia Station, the former heading for Willesden Junction or Stratford and the latter heading for Clapham Junction. This station used to have two through lines and two platform loops, but the original up loop and platform (seen behind the fence and now a garden) was closed before a new short platform was opened and then extended the length of the current up through line. Passenger numbers greatly increase when an event is held at the Exhibition Hall out of shot to the left. (*Fuji X-S1*)

8 January 2019. In low winter light, Freightliner 66 613 hauls its load of oil tanks out of Kensington Olympia Station, having passed through it on the middle through line. In the distance can be seen 378 203 just arriving at Platform 2, with a service for Clapham Junction. When passenger services all but ceased on the West London Line at the start of the Second World War, freight became its principal user and freight still continues to have a major presence on the route to this day. (*Canon 750d*)

19 March 2019. Clapham Junction-bound London Overground 378 203 has just closed its doors and is about to leave while Southern 377 208 pulls in alongside. Some Southern services terminate here and after running into a siding beyond the station (previously an access line into North Pole depot), come back into Shepherds Bush on the up line, while others continue towards Watford Junction. (*Canon 750d*)

27 January 2020. The 'new' Shepherds Bush national rail station on a cold wet night. The London Underground Central Line station bearing the same name is opposite on the left. The original station on this site was called Uxbridge Road and closed in 1940. The new station was opened in 2008 alongside the new Westfield shopping centre, seen on the left of the picture. (*Canon 750d*)

26 June 2020. A 378 crosses the Grand Union Canal section of Mitre Bridge. The bigger part of the bridge crosses the GWR Mainline out of shot on the right. Next stop will be Mitre Bridge Junction and then Willesden Junction. Though perhaps not as grand as the Kew Curve Grand Canal Bridge further down on the Richmond section of the North London Line, it still sees a lot of rail traffic. This stretch of the canal towpath is very popular with walkers and cyclists and the canal still sees river traffic. (*Canon 750d*)

Chapter Twelve

Willesden Junction

Willesden Junction Station is a bi-level station that sits to one side of a myriad of complex freight and passenger lines in northwest London. It is the interchange point between the Watford DC Lines, the North London Lines and the line to Clapham Junction via the West London Line. The Watford DC lines use the low-level station with the London Underground Bakerloo Line on Platforms 1 & 3. Platform 2 is a terminating bay platform used for Overground stock movement and special services. The North London and West London line join at Willesden High Level junction and use the high level station on Platforms 4 & 5 with some cross London freight trains. Willesden Junction is also the location for the London Overground depot that serves the Watford DC lines, North & West London and Gospel Oak to Barking lines, catering for class 378 and 710 EMUs. The main line platforms on the West Coast Mainline that run past the station closed in 1962.

11 August 2018. On a hot summers day, passengers can be seen descending the steps from the Harrow Road/A404 road bridge in the background, having just got off the bus as 378 234 approaches Platform 5 at Willesden Junction High Level station. Note the check rail inside the running rail because of the sharpness of the curve. (*Fuji X-S1*)

11 August 2018. No. 378 221 enters the Willesden Junction Traction Maintenance Depot, having just came off the Watford DC/Bakerloo lines, which continue past it towards Euston. It's passing brand new, recently delivered, Class 710s, awaiting their introduction into service. The line curving off bottom left is a link line connecting the Watford DC lines with the North London Line. (*Fuji X-S1*)

27 January 2020. A class 710 receives maintenance at Willesden Junction TMD around 8.30pm at night. By this time the software issues on the class 710s had been resolved, and the class had been rolled out on the Gospel Oak to Barking Line and were in large part replacing the 378s on the Watford DC lines. (*Canon 750d*)

11 August 2018. No. 378 209 leaves Platform 4 of Willesden High Level station, about to pass under the Harrow Road/A404 Bridge almost at midday. The footpath from the bridge to the station can be clearly seen. The tracks on the far right are the freight lines connecting the North London Line to the West Coast Mainline. (*Fuji X-S1*)

22 June 2020. Willesden Junction is a maze of walkways, subways and stairs joining the High and Low Level platforms. This building is the main station entrance now, often referred to as the North entrance. It's located on Station Approach, replacing an earlier building. This one was possibly built in 1999, when a new footbridge and lift was installed to serve the Low Level platforms. It also serves the high level platforms via a long walkway and a smaller original station building that acts as an entrance from the other direction. (*Canon 750d*)

8 December 2019. Although Network SouthEast ceased operations in 1994, its legacy can still be found in many places on the national railway network, due to its longevity. Here in the underpasses of Willesden Junction Station, the walls are still tiled in the red, white and blue of this much loved and much missed railway operator that ran this station and others on the North London lines from the '80s into the '90s. (*Canon 750d*)

11 August 2018. An interesting double headed Freightliner consisting of class 66 556 and an unidentified class 70 head through the site of the former Willesden Junction main line station on the West Coast Mainline. The platforms and station have long since been swept away after closing in 1962. In the background can be seen Willesden Junction TMD, with two new and recently delivered London Overground class 710 units sitting in the sidings. (*Fuji X-S1*)

26 June 2020. Two single track bridges carry the North London Line and West London Line over the West Coast Mainline. The one pictured is the up line towards Stratford with a class 378 passing over it. An identical bridge to the left carries the down line towards Clapham Junction and Richmond. These new spans replaced the original ones in 1976, which also accessed the mainline platforms below. These platforms were closed and removed in 1962 when the West Coast Mainline was electrified. (*Canon 750d*)

12 April 2019. No. 378 205 climbs the incline into Willesden Junction Low Level Station on the Watford DC Lines, having just traversed the tunnel under Harlesden Junction. Note the fourth rail used by London Underground Bakerloo Line trains that share this route with the Overground. A mostly empty Freightliner passes by in the opposite direction on the right, bound for the aforementioned junction to head onto the West Coast Main Line or for Wembley Yards. (*Canon 750d*)

12 April 2019. Willesden Low Level Station seen from the good vantage point of Old Oak Lane/A4000 road bridge. A 1972 London Underground Bakerloo line train waits to leave on the left to head into London, while London Overground 378 220 has just arrived on the right from Euston, to head up the Watford DC Line to Watford Junction. The little-used centre bay platform of the Low Level station can just be seen under the indenting in the awning. (*Canon 750d*)

12 April 2019. Brand new Bombardier class 710 (262) sits in the little used centre bay platform of Willesden Junction Low Level Station, about to engage in driver training and testing. Its indicator says 'Gospel Oak' and it will shortly leave here to travel to the Gospel Oak to Barking Line via the North London Line. Following soon behind it was its shadowing Europhoenix/ROG class 37 diesel locomotive on rescue duties should the need arise. (*Canon 750d*)

Chapter Thirteen

London Overground Signage

Being a part of Transport for London means London Overground shares a common brand identity with the London Underground, albeit with a change in colours from red and blue to orange and blue. The orange colour was apparently inherited from the East London Line when it was transferred from London Underground to London Overground. And like the Underground, the iconic roundel, created in 1908 with the 1913 Edward Johnston typeface, is instantly recognisable all over the world. The same applies for the route maps and the more traditional platform signs. All that has really changed is just the colour, to orange!

17 January 2010. In the days when London Overground took over from Silverlink Metro, many of the station signs were in a 'Temporary Orange'. Such an example could be found at Kensington Olympia during the changeover. The author has always wondered if the 'Temporary Sign' notice on the temporary sign was for the passengers or the marketing department? (*Sony A100*)

19 June 2020. It is said that the London Underground roundel above the entrance to Brixton Underground Station is the largest roundel on the TfL network. However, this one, located above the stairs going down into Dalston Junction Station from the concourse, must also be a contender. (*Canon 750d*)

20 April 2019. The Overground roundel at Wood Street Station on the Chingford Lea Valley branch amongst some nicely kept platform flower boxes. (*Fuji X-S1*)

9 June 2020. Though the majority of pictures used in this book were taken before the coronavirus pandemic of 2020, some of them were taken after travelling restrictions began to be relaxed, in order to complete the book by the deadline. These platform signs on the lamp posts and the platform surface urging 'social distancing' found at Imperial Wharf were common throughout the entire railway network. (*Canon 750d*)

19 November 2019. The signage may be clear, but many an unwitting passenger has run down the footbridge steps behind this photo and jumped onto the wrong Overground train in front of them! Confusion caused when Platforms 1 and 2 all but share the same platform face. (*Fuji X-S1*)

29 November 2019. TfL always takes November 11, Remembrance Sunday or Poppy Day as it's also known, very seriously, considering how many of its staff fought and died in two world wars. So every year it makes a special effort to adorn its trains, buses and roundels with the poppy motif associated with the First World War. This example was found at Edmonton Green, but others could also be found at other stations on the network. (*Canon 750d*)

29 November 2019. The borough of Waltham Forest was recognised as a London borough of culture in 2019 and various roundels at stations within Waltham Forest were adorned with this colourful roundel. This example was found at Highams Park, on the Chingford Branch of the Lea Valley Lines. (*Canon 750d*)

25 June 2020. While most platform signs on the Overground network take the shape and form of the iconic TfL roundel, in some places more traditional platform signs can also be found in the lengthwise format. This is such an example found at the platform ends of Silver Street, with the roundel also included. (*Canon 750d*)

6 July 2019. Like Poppy Day, the annual Gay Pride event is also widely celebrated across TfL and, like Poppy Day, the iconic TfL roundel gets similar treatment, this time, however, in the rainbow colours of the LGBT community. This one was found on Platform 1 at Romford on the Romford to Upminster Branch. (*Fuji X-S1*)

10 January 2020. Like Waltham Forest in 2019, the London Borough of Brent was named Borough of Cultures in 2020. And likewise, the TfL roundels at various stations within Brent were changed to reflect this status. This one was found at Willesden Junction on the Low Level platforms. (*Canon 750d*)

25 June 2020. The author's personal favourite is this handmade mosaic TfL roundel at Highams Park, made from glazed tiles in the colours of the Overground. It is quite simply a work of art! The brains behind it, the artist Maud Milton, working with others at her company Artyface, has also done others on the Lea Valley Lines, including at Chingford, South Tottenham and Leyton Midland Road. (*Canon 750d*)

25 June 2020. The traditional platform sign in Overground orange at Upminster Station on Platform 6, complete with route map below it. Most definitely the shortest route map on the whole of the London Overground network! (*Canon 750d*)

Chapter Fourteen

Overground Named Trains

A common tradition on Britain's railways has been to name various trains after people, events and places. The London Overground is no exception and has named a variety of its trains after people associated with the company and the Overground network. These are just some that the author has snapped on his travels in the process of creating this book.

Daks Hamilton

Ian Brown CBE

Professor Sir Peter Hall

Jeff Langston

Transport For London

The end for the last two Class 315s on London Overground came on 20th October 2020 when 315 807 and 802 forming an 8 car set, ran between Chingford, Liverpool Street, Enfield Town, Liverpool Street and back to Chingford one last time. During the day pens and badges were handed out by Overground staff as seen in the this photo, saying goodbye to the 315s and thanking them for nigh on 40 years of service. It was the end of an era.

Bibliography

Books
A Very Political Railway, Wayne Asher, Capital Transport, 2014.
An Enduring Legacy, East London Line Group 1990–2010, JRC Limited, 2010.
Branch Lines To Enfield Town & Palace Gates, J. E. Connor, Middleton Press, 2004.
Eastern Electric, John Glover, Ian Allan, 2003.
East London Line, Mitchell & Smith, Middleton Press, 1996.
Euston To Harrow & Wealdstone, K. Scholey, Middleton Press, 2002.
Harrow to Watford, Mitchell & Smith, Middleton Press, 2003.
History of the North London Railway Vol.1, Atkinson/Adams & Clark. North London Railway Historical Society, 2015.
Liverpool Street to Chingford, J. E. Connor, Middleton Press, 2003.
London's Branch Railways, John Glover, Ian Allan Publishing, 1999.
London Bridge to East Croydon, Mitchell & Smith, Middleton Press, 1988.
London's Overground, John Glover, Ian Allan, 2012.
London Railway Atlas, Joe Brown, Ian Allan, Various Editions.
London's Railway Heritage Vol.3: North GER, Peter Kay, 2015.
Network SouthEast, Mark Lawrence, OPC, 1994.
North London Line, Mitchell & Smith, Middleton Press, 1997.
Railway Track Diagrams 5: England South & London Underground, Quail Map Company.
South London Line, Mitchell & Smith, Middleton Press, 1995.
St Pancras to Barking, J. E. Connor, Middleton Press, 2005.
Tilbury Loop, Dr E. Course, Middleton Press, 2002.
The Network SouthEast Story, Green & Vincent, OPC, 2014.
The North London Railway 1846–2001, Dennis Lovett, Irwell Press, 2001.
The Tottenham Joint Lines, J. E. Connor, Connor and Butler, 1993.
The West London Joint Railways, J. B. Atkinson, Ian Allan Publishing, 1984.
West London Line, Mitchell & Smith, Middleton Press, 1996.
Willesden Junction to Richmond, Mitchell & Smith, Middleton Press, 1996.

DVDs
East London Line & New South London Line (225 Studios).
Euston To Watford Junction & Return (225 Studios).
Gospel Oak To Barking & Return & Clapham Jn (225 Studios).
Stratford to Richmond & Return (225 Studios).
City Lines Remembered (Online Video.)
Eastern Region Journey (Transport Video Publishing).
East London Line – Past and Present (J&K Video).
London Overground Lea Valley Lines & TfL Rail (J&K Video).
London Overground Gospel Oak to Barking (J&K Video).
London Overground – North London Line (J&K Video).